Born Blessed

280 Declarations for the Child

Bozena Ryt *and* Olivia Ryt

WESTBOW
PRESS®
A DIVISION OF THOMAS NELSON
& ZONDERVAN

WestBow Press books may be ordered through booksellers or by contacting:

WestBow Press
A Division of Thomas Nelson & Zondervan
1663 Liberty Drive
Bloomington, IN 47403
www.westbowpress.com
844-714-3454

ISBN: 978-1-6642-7613-0 (sc)
ISBN: 978-1-6642-7615-4 (hc)
ISBN: 978-1-6642-7614-7 (e)

Library of Congress Control Number: 2022915584

Print information available on the last page.

WestBow Press rev. date: 9/22/2022

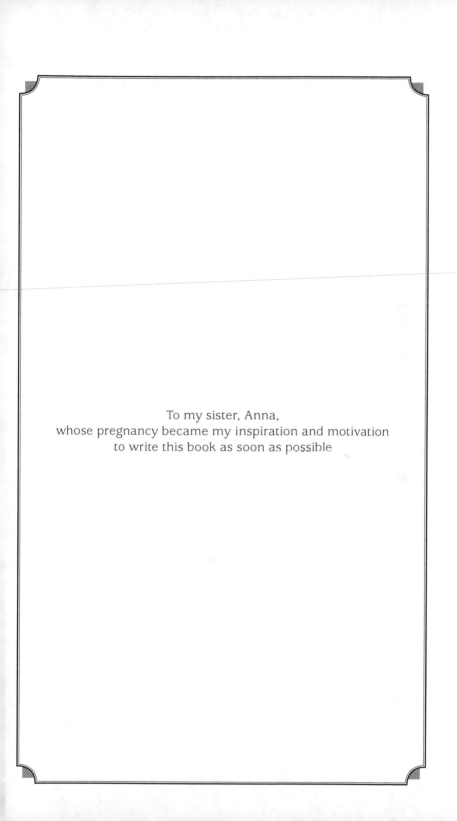

To my sister, Anna,
whose pregnancy became my inspiration and motivation
to write this book as soon as possible

How to Use This Book

This book is for every pregnant woman and every person who wants to bless her or his baby. Although it was written specially for pregnant women, we encourage expecting fathers to bless their babies every day as well. The book can also be used by people who have never been blessed by their parents—you can bless yourself now.

The book offers 280 days of declarations, one for each day of a typical pregnancy of forty weeks. Each day, read one declaration and declare it over your child. You can declare as many times as you want, until it sinks into your spirit.

Each day includes the scripture on which the declaration was based. At the end of each day, you can add a *Magnificat*. It's up to you.

When the text refers to *my baby*, you can read it as is or fill in the name of your child. You can also use the declarations for your adult children.

Remember, God's time is not our time.
God is your Father.

Magnificat

And Mary said:
"My soul magnifies the Lord,
　　　and my spirit rejoices in God my Savior,
for he has looked with favor on the lowliness of his servant.
　　　Surely, from now on all generations will call me
　　　blessed;
for the Mighty One has done great things for me,
　　　and holy is his name.
His mercy is for those who fear him
　　　from generation to generation.
He has shown strength with his arm;
　　　he has scattered the proud in the thoughts of their
　　　hearts.
He has brought down the powerful from their thrones,
　　　and lifted up the lowly;
he has filled the hungry with good things,
　　　and sent the rich away empty.
He has helped his servant Israel,
　　　in remembrance of his mercy,
according to the promise he made to our ancestors,
　　　to Abraham and to his descendants forever."

Luke 1:46–55 (NRSV)

Day 1

Before Father God, I decree, and I declare in the name of Jesus Christ of Nazareth, that you, *my baby*,[1] are God's child, and God will fully supply whatever you need, in accord with His glorious riches in Christ Jesus.

Thank You, Father. I praise You, Father. I worship You, Father. Thank You, Jesus. I praise You, Jesus. I worship You, Jesus. Thank You, Holy Spirit. I praise You, Holy Spirit. I worship You, Holy Spirit.
Amen.

> My God will fully supply whatever you need,
> in accord with his glorious riches in Christ Jesus.
> Philippians 4:19

Day 2

Before Father God I decree, and I declare in the name of Jesus Christ of Nazareth, that you, *my baby*, have the strength for everything through Him who empowers you.

Thank You, Father. I praise You, Father. I worship You, Father. Thank You, Jesus. I praise You, Jesus. I worship You, Jesus. Thank You, Holy Spirit. I praise You, Holy Spirit. I worship You, Holy Spirit.
Amen.

> I have the strength for everything
> through him who empowers me.
> Philippians 4:13

---

[1] Remember that you can speak your child's name or just say "my baby." If you are declaring for yourself, you can leave out "my baby" or insert your own name.

Day 3

Before Father God I decree, and I declare in the name of Jesus Christ of Nazareth, that you, *my baby*, are the perfect gift from above, coming down to me, to all people, from the Father of Lights, with whom there is no alteration or shadow caused by change.

Thank You, Father. I praise You, Father. I worship You, Father. Thank You, Jesus. I praise You, Jesus. I worship You, Jesus. Thank You, Holy Spirit. I praise You, Holy Spirit. I worship You, Holy Spirit.
Amen.

> All good giving and every perfect gift is from above,
> coming down from the Father of lights, with whom
> there is no alteration or shadow caused by change.
> James 1:17

Day 4

Before Father God I decree, and I declare in the name of Jesus Christ of Nazareth, that you, *my baby*, received birth from God by the Word of Truth that you may be a kind of firstfruits of his creatures.

Thank You, Father. I praise You, Father. I worship You, Father. Thank You, Jesus. I praise You, Jesus. I worship You, Jesus. Thank You, Holy Spirit. I praise You, Holy Spirit. I worship You, Holy Spirit.
Amen.

> He willed to give us birth by the word
> of truth that we may be
> a kind of firstfruits of his creatures.
> James 1:18

Day 5

Before Father God I decree, and I declare in the name of Jesus Christ of Nazareth, that you, *my baby*, will not fear, because God is with you. You will not be anxious, because God is your God. He will strengthen you. He will help you. He will uphold you with His victorious right hand.

Thank You, Father. I praise You, Father. I worship You, Father. Thank You, Jesus. I praise You, Jesus. I worship You, Jesus. Thank You, Holy Spirit. I praise You, Holy Spirit. I worship You, Holy Spirit.
Amen.

> Do not fear. I am with you;
> do not be anxious: I am your God.
> I will strengthen you, I will help you,
> I will uphold you with my victorious right hand.
> Isaiah 41:10

Day 6

Before Father God I decree, and I declare in the name of Jesus Christ of Nazareth, that you, *my baby*, have grace and peace from God our Father and the Lord Jesus Christ.

Thank You, Father. I praise You, Father. I worship You, Father. Thank You, Jesus. I praise You, Jesus. I worship You, Jesus. Thank You, Holy Spirit. I praise You, Holy Spirit. I worship You, Holy Spirit.
Amen.

> Grace to you and peace from God our
> Father and the Lord Jesus Christ.
> Galatians 1:3

Day 7

Before Father God I decree, and I declare in the name of Jesus Christ of Nazareth, that you, *my baby*, are called by God through His grace, and God is pleased to reveal to you His Son, that you might proclaim Him to the nations.

Thank You, Father. I praise You, Father. I worship You, Father. Thank You, Jesus. I praise You, Jesus. I worship You, Jesus. Thank You, Holy Spirit. I praise You, Holy Spirit. I worship You, Holy Spirit.
Amen.

> But when [God], who from my mother's womb had
> set me apart and called me through his grace,
> was pleased to reveal his Son to me, so that
> I might proclaim him to the Gentiles,
> I did not immediately consult flesh and blood.
> Galatians 1:15

Day 8

Before Father God I decree, and I declare in the name of Jesus Christ of Nazareth, that you, *my baby*, received His fullness, grace in place of grace. Grace and truth came to you through Jesus Christ.

Thank You, Father. I praise You, Father. I worship You, Father. Thank You, Jesus. I praise You, Jesus. I worship You, Jesus. Thank You, Holy Spirit. I praise You, Holy Spirit. I worship You, Holy Spirit.
Amen.

> From his fullness we have all received,
> grace in place of grace,
> because while the law was given through Moses,
> grace and truth came through Jesus Christ.
> John 1:16–17

Day 9

Before Father God I decree, and I declare in the name of Jesus Christ of Nazareth, that you, *my baby*, are blessed by God and your descendants will be as countless as the stars of the sky and the sands of the seashore.

Thank You, Father. I praise You, Father. I worship You, Father. Thank You, Jesus. I praise You, Jesus. I worship You, Jesus. Thank You, Holy Spirit. I praise You, Holy Spirit. I worship You, Holy Spirit.
Amen.

> I will bless you and make your descendants as countless as the stars of the sky and the sands of the seashore.
> Genesis 22:17

Day 10

Before Father God I decree, and I declare in the name of Jesus Christ of Nazareth, that you, *my baby*, are blessed. May God give you heaven's dew, earth's richness, and abundance of grain and wine.

Thank You, Father. I praise You, Father. I worship You, Father. Thank You, Jesus. I praise You, Jesus. I worship You, Jesus. Thank You, Holy Spirit. I praise You, Holy Spirit. I worship You, Holy Spirit.
Amen.

> May God give to you
> of the dew of the heavens
> And of fertility of the earth
> abundance of grain and wine.
> Genesis 27:28

Day 11

Before Father God I decree, and I declare in the name of Jesus Christ of Nazareth, that you, *my baby*, are a new creation in Christ.

Thank You, Father. I praise You, Father. I worship You, Father. Thank You, Jesus. I praise You, Jesus. I worship You, Jesus. Thank You, Holy Spirit. I praise You, Holy Spirit. I worship You, Holy Spirit.
Amen.

> So whoever is in Christ is a new creation:
> the old things have passed away;
> behold, new things have come.
> 2 Corinthians 5:17

Day 12

Before Father God I decree, and I declare in the name of Jesus Christ of Nazareth, that you, *my baby*, are an ambassador for Christ.

Thank You, Father. I praise You, Father. I worship You, Father. Thank You, Jesus. I praise You, Jesus. I worship You, Jesus. Thank You, Holy Spirit. I praise You, Holy Spirit. I worship You, Holy Spirit.
Amen.

> So, we are ambassadors for Christ, as if
> God were appealing through us.
> We implore you on behalf of Christ, be reconciled to God.
> 2 Corinthians 5:20

Day 13

Before Father God I decree, and I declare in the name of Jesus Christ of Nazareth, that you, my baby, are the righteousness of God in Christ.

Thank You, Father. I praise You, Father. I worship You, Father. Thank You, Jesus. I praise You, Jesus. I worship You, Jesus. Thank You, Holy Spirit. I praise You, Holy Spirit. I worship You, Holy Spirit.
Amen.

For our sake he made him to be sin who did not know sin, so that we might become the righteousness of God in him.
2 Corinthians 5:21

Day 14

Before Father God I decree, and I declare in the name of Jesus Christ of Nazareth, that you, *my baby,* will delight in the law of the Lord and the law of the Lord will be your joy. You will meditate on the Lord's law day and night.

Thank You, Father. I praise You, Father. I worship You, Father. Thank You, Jesus. I praise You, Jesus. I worship You, Jesus. Thank You, Holy Spirit. I praise You, Holy Spirit. I worship You, Holy Spirit.
Amen.

Blessed is the man who does not walk
in the counsel of the wicked,
nor stand in the way of sinners,
nor sit in company with scoffers.
Rather, the law of the Lord is his joy;
and on his law he meditates day and night.
Psalm 1:1–2

Day 15

Before Father God I decree, and I declare in the name of Jesus Christ of Nazareth, that you, *my baby*, are like a tree planted near streams of water that yields its fruit in season. Your leaves will never wither; whatever you do prospers.

Thank You, Father. I praise You, Father. I worship You, Father. Thank You, Jesus. I praise You, Jesus. I worship You, Jesus. Thank You, Holy Spirit. I praise You, Holy Spirit. I worship You, Holy Spirit.
Amen.

> He is like a tree
> planted near streams of water,
> that yields its fruit in season;
> Its leaves never wither,
> whatever he does prospers.
> Psalm 1:3

Day 16

Before Father God I decree, and I declare in the name of Jesus Christ of Nazareth, that you, *my baby*, are God's beloved and cherished child. You are born by God's decision. God gave you power to become His child.

Thank You, Father. I praise You, Father. I worship You, Father. Thank You, Jesus. I praise You, Jesus. I worship You, Jesus. Thank You, Holy Spirit. I praise You, Holy Spirit. I worship You, Holy Spirit.
Amen.

> But those who did accept him he gave
> power to become children of God,
> to those who believe in his name, who
> were born not by natural generation
> nor by human choice nor by a man's decision but of God.
> John 1:12

Day 17

Before Father God I decree, and I declare in the name of Jesus Christ of Nazareth, that you, *my baby*, are loved by God. He is your shepherd; you lack nothing. In green pastures He makes you lie down next to still waters. He leads you and He restores you.

Thank You, Father. I praise You, Father. I worship You, Father. Thank You, Jesus. I praise You, Jesus. I worship You, Jesus. Thank You, Holy Spirit. I praise You, Holy Spirit. I worship You, Holy Spirit.
Amen.

> The LORD is my shepherd;
> there is nothing I lack.
> In green pastures he makes me lie down;
> to still waters he leads me
> he restores my soul.
> He guides me along paths
> for the sake of his name.
> Psalm 23:1–2

Day 18

Before Father God I decree, and I declare in the name of Jesus Christ of Nazareth, that you, *my baby*, have courage; you are with God, His rod and staff comfort you.

Thank You, Father. I praise You, Father. I worship You, Father. Thank You, Jesus. I praise You, Jesus. I worship You, Jesus. Thank You, Holy Spirit. I praise You, Holy Spirit. I worship You, Holy Spirit.
Amen.

> Even though I walk through the valley of the shadow of death,
> I will fear no evil, for you are with me;
> your rod and your staff comfort me.
> Psalm 23:4

Day 19

Before Father God I decree, and I declare in the name of Jesus Christ of Nazareth, that you, *my baby*, are anointed. Your head is anointed with oil; your cup overflows. Goodness and mercy will pursue you all the days of your life. You will dwell in the house of the Lord for endless days.

Thank You, Father. I praise You, Father. I worship You, Father. Thank You, Jesus. I praise You, Jesus. I worship You, Jesus. Thank You, Holy Spirit. I praise You, Holy Spirit. I worship You, Holy Spirit.
Amen.

> You set a table before me
> in front of my enemies;
> You anoint my head with oil;
> my cup overflows.
> Indeed, goodness and mercy will pursue me
> all the days of my life;
> I will dwell in the house of the LORD
> for endless days.
> Psalm 23:5–6

Day 20

Before Father God I decree, and I declare in the name of Jesus Christ of Nazareth, that you, *my baby*, are the Bride of Christ.

Thank You, Father. I praise You, Father. I worship You, Father. Thank You, Jesus. I praise You, Jesus. I worship You, Jesus. Thank You, Holy Spirit. I praise You, Holy Spirit. I worship You, Holy Spirit.
Amen.

> Let us rejoice and be glad
> and give him glory.
> For the wedding day of the Lamb has come,
> his bride has made herself ready.
> Revelation 19:7

Day 21

Before Father God I decree, and I declare in the name of Jesus Christ of Nazareth, that you, *my baby*, will say that the Lord is your rock, your fortress, your deliverer. The Lord is your shield, your saving horn, your stronghold, your refuge, your Savior.

Thank You, Father. I praise You, Father. I worship You, Father. Thank You, Jesus. I praise You, Jesus. I worship You, Jesus. Thank You, Holy Spirit. I praise You, Holy Spirit. I worship You, Holy Spirit.
Amen.

He [David] said:
O LORD, my rock, my fortress, my deliverer,
my God, my rock of refuge!
My shield, my saving horn,
my stronghold, my refuge,
my savior, from violence you keep me safe.
2 Samuel 22:2–3

Day 22

Before Father God I decree, and I declare in the name of Jesus Christ of Nazareth, that you, *my baby*, are no longer a slave but a child, and if a child then also an heir through God.

Thank You, Father. I praise You, Father. I worship You, Father. Thank You, Jesus. I praise You, Jesus. I worship You, Jesus. Thank You, Holy Spirit. I praise You, Holy Spirit. I worship You, Holy Spirit.
Amen.

So, you are no longer a slave but a child, and
if a child then also an heir, through God.
Galatians 4:7

Day 23

Before Father God I decree, and I declare in the name of Jesus Christ of Nazareth, that you, *my baby*, are abundant in every grace; you always have all you need, and an abundance for every good work.

Thank You, Father. I praise You, Father. I worship You, Father. Thank You, Jesus. I praise You, Jesus. I worship You, Jesus. Thank You, Holy Spirit. I praise You, Holy Spirit. I worship You, Holy Spirit.
Amen.

Moreover, God is able to make every
grace abundant for you,
so that in all things, always having all you need, you
may have an abundance for every good work.
2 Corinthians 9:8

Day 24

Before Father God I decree, and I declare in the name of Jesus Christ of Nazareth, that you, *my baby*, have a home where God's righteousness endures forever.

Thank You, Father. I praise You, Father. I worship You, Father. Thank You, Jesus. I praise You, Jesus. I worship You, Jesus. Thank You, Holy Spirit. I praise You, Holy Spirit. I worship You, Holy Spirit.
Amen.

As it is written:
"He scatters abroad, he gives to the poor:
his righteousness endures forever."
2 Corinthians 9:9

Day 25

Before Father God I decree, and I declare in the name of Jesus Christ of Nazareth, that you, *my baby*, have all the seeds that you need. God will supply and multiply your seed and increase the harvest of your righteousness.

Thank You, Father. I praise You, Father. I worship You, Father. Thank You, Jesus. I praise You, Jesus. I worship You, Jesus. Thank You, Holy Spirit. I praise You, Holy Spirit. I worship You, Holy Spirit.
Amen.

The one who supplies seed to the sower and bread for food
will supply and multiply your seed and increase
the harvest of your righteousness.
2 Corinthians 9:10

Day 26

Before Father God I decree, and I declare in the name of Jesus Christ of Nazareth, that you, *my baby*, are part of God's glorious church. You are holy, without blemish.

Thank You, Father. I praise You, Father. I worship You, Father. Thank You, Jesus. I praise You, Jesus. I worship You, Jesus. Thank You, Holy Spirit. I praise You, Holy Spirit. I worship You, Holy Spirit.
Amen.

Husbands love your wives, even as Christ loved the church
and handed himself over for her to sanctify her,
cleansing her by the bath of water with the word,
that he might present to himself to church in splendor,
without spot or wrinkle or any such thing,
that she might be holy and without blemish.
Ephesians 5:25-27

Day 27

Before Father God I decree, and I declare in the name of Jesus Christ of Nazareth, that you, *my baby*, have the peace of God that surpasses all understanding. Peace of God will guard your heart and mind in Jesus Christ.

Thank You, Father. I praise You, Father. I worship You, Father. Thank You, Jesus. I praise You, Jesus. I worship You, Jesus. Thank You, Holy Spirit. I praise You, Holy Spirit. I worship You, Holy Spirit.
Amen.

Then the peace of God that surpasses all understanding
will guard your hearts and minds in Christ Jesus.
Philippians 4:7

Day 28

Before Father God I decree, and I declare in the name of Jesus Christ of Nazareth, that you, *my baby*, have no anxiety at all, but in everything, by prayer and petition, with thanksgiving, make your request known to God.

Thank You, Father. I praise You, Father. I worship You, Father. Thank You, Jesus. I praise You, Jesus. I worship You, Jesus. Thank You, Holy Spirit. I praise You, Holy Spirit. I worship You, Holy Spirit.
Amen.

Have no anxiety at all, but in everything,
by prayer and petition,
with thanksgiving, make your request known to God.
Philippians 4:6

Day 29

Before Father God I decree, and I declare in the name of Jesus Christ of Nazareth, that you, *my baby*, are the light of the world.

Thank You, Father. I praise You, Father. I worship You, Father. Thank You, Jesus. I praise You, Jesus. I worship You, Jesus. Thank You, Holy Spirit. I praise You, Holy Spirit. I worship You, Holy Spirit.
Amen.

You are the light of the world. A city set
on a mountain cannot be hidden.
Matthew 5:14

Day 30

Before Father God I decree, and I declare in the name of Jesus Christ of Nazareth, that you, *my baby*, will remember the Lord. From the Lord you have received power to get wealth.

Thank You, Father. I praise You, Father. I worship You, Father. Thank You, Jesus. I praise You, Jesus. I worship You, Jesus. Thank You, Holy Spirit. I praise You, Holy Spirit. I worship You, Holy Spirit.
Amen.

Remember then the LORD, your God,
for he is the one who gives you
the power to get wealth, by fulfilling, as he has now done,
the covenant he swore to your ancestors.
Deuteronomy 8:18

Day 31

Before Father God I decree, and I declare in the name of Jesus Christ of Nazareth, that you, *my baby*, are the salt of the earth.

Thank You, Father. I praise You, Father. I worship You, Father. Thank You, Jesus. I praise You, Jesus. I worship You, Jesus. Thank You, Holy Spirit. I praise You, Holy Spirit. I worship You, Holy Spirit.
Amen.

> You are the salt of the earth. But if salt loses its taste,
> with what can it be seasoned? It is
> no longer good for anything
> but to be thrown out and trampled underfoot.
> Matthew 5:13

Day 32

Before Father God I decree, and I declare in the name of Jesus Christ of Nazareth, that you, *my baby*, have happy and blessed eyes because they see, and you have happy and blessed ears because they hear.

Thank You, Father. I praise You, Father. I worship You, Father. Thank You, Jesus. I praise You, Jesus. I worship You, Jesus. Thank You, Holy Spirit. I praise You, Holy Spirit. I worship You, Holy Spirit.
Amen.

> But blessed are your eyes, because they see,
> and your ears, because they hear.
> Matthew 13:16

Day 33

Before Father God I decree, and I declare in the name of Jesus Christ of Nazareth, that you, *my baby*, are Christ's pearl of great price.

Thank You, Father. I praise You, Father. I worship You, Father. Thank You, Jesus. I praise You, Jesus. I worship You, Jesus. Thank You, Holy Spirit. I praise You, Holy Spirit. I worship You, Holy Spirit.
Amen.

When he finds a pearl of great price, he goes
and sells all that he has and buys it.
Matthew 13:46

Day 34

Before Father God I decree, and I declare in the name of Jesus Christ of Nazareth, that you, *my baby*, are blessed because you trust the Lord and the Lord is your trust.

Thank You, Father. I praise You, Father. I worship You, Father. Thank You, Jesus. I praise You, Jesus. I worship You, Jesus. Thank You, Holy Spirit. I praise You, Holy Spirit. I worship You, Holy Spirit.
Amen.

Blessed are those who trust in the LORD;
the LORD will be their trust.
Jeremiah 17:7

Day 35

Before Father God I decree, and I declare in the name of Jesus Christ of Nazareth, that you, *my baby*, are fertile and you will multiply. You will fill the earth and subdue it. You have dominion over the fish of the sea, the birds of the air, and all the living things that crawl on the earth.

Thank You, Father. I praise You, Father. I worship You, Father. Thank You, Jesus. I praise You, Jesus. I worship You, Jesus. Thank You, Holy Spirit. I praise You, Holy Spirit. I worship You, Holy Spirit.
Amen.

God blessed them and God said to them:
Be fertile and multiply, fill the earth and subdue it.
Have dominion over the fish of the sea, the birds of the air,
and all the living things that crawl on the earth.
Genesis 1:28

Day 36

Before Father God I decree, and I declare in the name of Jesus Christ of Nazareth, that you, *my baby*, have every seed-bearing plant on the earth and every tree that has seed bearing fruit.

Thank You, Father. I praise You, Father. I worship You, Father. Thank You, Jesus. I praise You, Jesus. I worship You, Jesus. Thank You, Holy Spirit. I praise You, Holy Spirit. I worship You, Holy Spirit.
Amen.

God also said See, I give you every seed-
bearing plant on all the earth
and every tree that has seed-bearing fruit on it to be your food,
and to all the wild animals and all the birds
of the air and all the living creatures
that crawl on the earth, I give all the green plants for food.
And so it happened.
Genesis 1:29–30

Day 37

Before Father God I decree, and I declare in the name of Jesus Christ of Nazareth, that you, *my baby*, have power to build up.

Thank You, Father. I praise You, Father. I worship You, Father. Thank You, Jesus. I praise You, Jesus. I worship You, Jesus. Thank You, Holy Spirit. I praise You, Holy Spirit. I worship You, Holy Spirit.
Amen.

I am writing this while I am away, so that when
I come I may not have to be severe in virtue
of the authority that the Lord has given me
to build up and not to tear down.
2 Corinthians 13:10

Day 38

Before Father God I decree, and I declare in the name of Jesus Christ of Nazareth, that you, *my baby*, have received the grace of the Lord Jesus Christ, the love of God, and the fellowship of the Holy Spirit.

Thank You, Father. I praise You, Father. I worship You, Father. Thank You, Jesus. I praise You, Jesus. I worship You, Jesus. Thank You, Holy Spirit. I praise You, Holy Spirit. I worship You, Holy Spirit.
Amen.

The grace of the Lord Jesus Christ and the love of God
and the fellowship of the Holy Spirit be with all of you.
2 Corinthians 13:13

Day 39

Before Father God I decree, and I declare in the name of Jesus Christ of Nazareth, that you, *my baby*, are the temple of the living God.

Thank You, Father. I praise You, Father. I worship You, Father. Thank You, Jesus. I praise You, Jesus. I worship You, Jesus. Thank You, Holy Spirit. I praise You, Holy Spirit. I worship You, Holy Spirit.
Amen.

> What agreement has the temple of God with idols? For
> we are the temple of the living God; as God said:
> "I will live with them and move among them,
> and I will be their God
> and they shall be my people."
> 2 Corinthians 6:16

Day 40

Before Father God I decree, and I declare in the name of Jesus Christ of Nazareth, that you, *my baby*, will seek first the kingdom of God and His righteousness, and all things will be given you besides.

Thank You, Father. I praise You, Father. I worship You, Father. Thank You, Jesus. I praise You, Jesus. I worship You, Jesus. Thank You, Holy Spirit. I praise You, Holy Spirit. I worship You, Holy Spirit.
Amen.

> But seek first the kingdom [of God] and his righteousness,
> and all these things will be given you besides.
> Matthew 6:33

Day 41

Before Father God I decree, and I declare in the name of Jesus Christ of Nazareth, that you, *my baby*, are more than a conqueror through Jesus who loves you.

Thank You, Father. I praise You, Father. I worship You, Father. Thank You, Jesus. I praise You, Jesus. I worship You, Jesus. Thank You, Holy Spirit. I praise You, Holy Spirit. I worship You, Holy Spirit.
Amen.

> No, in all these things we conquer
> overwhelmingly through him who loved us.
> Romans 8:37

Day 42

Before Father God I decree, and I declare in the name of Jesus Christ of Nazareth, that you, *my baby*, are redeemed.

Thank You, Father. I praise You, Father. I worship You, Father. Thank You, Jesus. I praise You, Jesus. I worship You, Jesus. Thank You, Holy Spirit. I praise You, Holy Spirit. I worship You, Holy Spirit.
Amen.

> They sang a new hymn:
> "Worthy are you to receive the scroll
> and to break open its seals,
> for you were for you were slain and with
> your blood you purchased for God
> those from every tribe and tongue, people and nation."
> Revelation 5:9

Day 43

Before Father God I decree, and I declare in the name of Jesus Christ of Nazareth, that you, *my baby*, are an overcomer. You will overcome everything with Jesus's blood.

Thank You, Father. I praise You, Father. I worship You, Father. Thank You, Jesus. I praise You, Jesus. I worship You, Jesus. Thank You, Holy Spirit. I praise You, Holy Spirit. I worship You, Holy Spirit.
Amen.

> They conquered him by the blood of the Lamb
> and by the word of their testimony;
> love for life did not deter them from death.
> Revelation 12:11

Day 44

Before Father God I decree, and I declare in the name of Jesus Christ of Nazareth, that you, *my baby*, are blessed in Christ with every spiritual blessing in the heavens.

Thank You, Father. I praise You, Father. I worship You, Father. Thank You, Jesus. I praise You, Jesus. I worship You, Jesus. Thank You, Holy Spirit. I praise You, Holy Spirit. I worship You, Holy Spirit.
Amen.

> Blessed be the God and Father of our Lord Jesus Christ,
> who has blessed us in Christ with every
> spiritual blessing in the heavens.
> Ephesians 1:3

Day 45

Before Father God I decree, and I declare in the name of Jesus Christ of Nazareth, that you, *my baby*, were chosen in Jesus Christ before the foundation of the world, to be holy and without blemish before Him.

Thank You, Father. I praise You, Father. I worship You, Father.
Thank You, Jesus. I praise You, Jesus. I worship You, Jesus.
Thank You, Holy Spirit. I praise You, Holy Spirit. I worship You, Holy Spirit.
Amen.

> Blessed be the God and Father of our Lord
> Jesus Christ, ... as he chose us in him,
> before the foundation of the world, to be
> holy and without blemish before him.
> Ephesians 1:3–4

Day 46

Before Father God I decree, and I declare in the name of Jesus Christ of Nazareth, that you, *my baby*, were predestined in love, determined by God. You are adopted by God through Jesus Christ. You are God's child.

Thank You, Father. I praise You, Father. I worship You, Father.
Thank You, Jesus. I praise You, Jesus. I worship You, Jesus.
Thank You, Holy Spirit. I praise You, Holy Spirit. I worship You, Holy Spirit.
Amen.

> In love he destined us for adoption to
> himself through Jesus Christ,
> in accord with the favor of his will.
> Ephesians 1:4–5

Day 47

Before Father God I decree, and I declare in the name of Jesus Christ of Nazareth, that you, *my baby*, were chosen in Him. You were destined in accord with the purpose of the One who accomplishes all things according to the intention of His will.

Thank You, Father. I praise You, Father. I worship You, Father. Thank You, Jesus. I praise You, Jesus. I worship You, Jesus. Thank You, Holy Spirit. I praise You, Holy Spirit. I worship You, Holy Spirit.
Amen.

> In him we were also chosen, destined in
> accord with the purpose of the One
> who accomplishes all things according
> to the intention of his will.
> Ephesians 1:11

Day 48

Before Father God I decree, and I declare in the name of Jesus Christ of Nazareth, that you, *my baby*, were sealed with the Holy Spirit.

Thank You, Father. I praise You, Father. I worship You, Father. Thank You, Jesus. I praise You, Jesus. I worship You, Jesus. Thank You, Holy Spirit. I praise You, Holy Spirit. I worship You, Holy Spirit.
Amen.

> In him you also, who have heard the word
> of truth, the gospel of your salvation,
> and have believed in him, were sealed
> with the promised holy Spirit.
> Ephesians 1:13

Day 49

Before Father God I decree, and I declare in the name of Jesus Christ of Nazareth, that you, *my baby*, have inherited the Holy Spirit.

Thank You, Father. I praise You, Father. I worship You, Father. Thank You, Jesus. I praise You, Jesus. I worship You, Jesus. Thank You, Holy Spirit. I praise You, Holy Spirit. I worship You, Holy Spirit.
Amen.

> The promised Holy Spirit ... is the first
> installment of our inheritance
> toward redemption as God's possession.
> Ephesians 1:13–14

Day 50

Before Father God I decree, and I declare in the name of Jesus Christ of Nazareth, that you, *my baby*, have the spirit of wisdom and revelation.

Thank You, Father. I praise You, Father. I worship You, Father. Thank You, Jesus. I praise You, Jesus. I worship You, Jesus. Thank You, Holy Spirit. I praise You, Holy Spirit. I worship You, Holy Spirit.
Amen.

> Therefore, I, too, ... do not cease giving thanks
> for you, remembering you in my prayers,
> that the God of our Lord Jesus Christ, the Father of glory,
> may give you a spirit of wisdom and revelation .
> Ephesians 1:15–17

Day 51

Before Father God I decree, and I declare in the name of Jesus Christ of Nazareth, that you, *my baby*, know the riches of the glory of God.

Thank You, Father. I praise You, Father. I worship You, Father. Thank You, Jesus. I praise You, Jesus. I worship You, Jesus. Thank You, Holy Spirit. I praise You, Holy Spirit. I worship You, Holy Spirit.
Amen.

> May the eyes of your hearts be
> enlightened, that you may know
> what is the hope that belongs to his call,
> what are the riches of glory in his
> inheritance among the holy ones.
> Ephesians 1:18

Day 52

Before Father God I decree, and I declare in the name of Jesus Christ of Nazareth, that you, *my baby*, received God's power because you believe, in accord of His great might.

Thank You, Father. I praise You, Father. I worship You, Father. Thank You, Jesus. I praise You, Jesus. I worship You, Jesus. Thank You, Holy Spirit. I praise You, Holy Spirit. I worship You, Holy Spirit.
Amen.

> And what is the surpassing greatness of
> his power for us who believe,
> in accord with the exercise of his great might.
> Ephesians 1:19

Day 53

Before Father God I decree, and I declare in the name of Jesus Christ of Nazareth, that you, *my baby*, are alive with Christ. You have been saved by grace.

Thank You, Father. I praise You, Father. I worship You, Father. Thank You, Jesus. I praise You, Jesus. I worship You, Jesus. Thank You, Holy Spirit. I praise You, Holy Spirit. I worship You, Holy Spirit.
Amen.

But God … even when we were dead in our transgressions
brought us alive with Christ, (by
grace you have been saved).
Ephesians 2:4–5

Day 54

Before Father God I decree, and I declare in the name of Jesus Christ of Nazareth, that you, *my baby*, are raised up and seated with Christ in the heavens.

Thank You, Father. I praise You, Father. I worship You, Father. Thank You, Jesus. I praise You, Jesus. I worship You, Jesus. Thank You, Holy Spirit. I praise You, Holy Spirit. I worship You, Holy Spirit.
Amen.

[God] raised us up with him, and seated us
with him in the heavens in Christ Jesus.
Ephesians 2:6

Day 55

Before Father God I decree, and I declare in the name of Jesus Christ of Nazareth, that you, *my baby*, have received immeasurable richness of God's grace in His kindness to us in Christ Jesus.

Thank You, Father. I praise You, Father. I worship You, Father. Thank You, Jesus. I praise You, Jesus. I worship You, Jesus. Thank You, Holy Spirit. I praise You, Holy Spirit. I worship You, Holy Spirit.
Amen.

> That in the ages to come he might show the
> immeasurable richness of his grace
> in his kindness to us in Christ Jesus.
> Ephesians 2:7

Day 56

Before Father God I decree, and I declare in the name of Jesus Christ of Nazareth, that you, *my baby*, have been saved by grace through faith. Grace is a gift from God.

Thank You, Father. I praise You, Father. I worship You, Father. Thank You, Jesus. I praise You, Jesus. I worship You, Jesus. Thank You, Holy Spirit. I praise You, Holy Spirit. I worship You, Holy Spirit.
Amen.

> For by grace you have been saved through faith
> and this is not from you; it is the gift of God.
> Ephesians 2:8

Day 57

Before Father God I decree, and I declare in the name of Jesus Christ of Nazareth, that you, *my baby*, are God's handiwork. You are created in Christ Jesus for the good works that God has prepared in advance that you should live in Him.

Thank You, Father. I praise You, Father. I worship You, Father. Thank You, Jesus. I praise You, Jesus. I worship You, Jesus. Thank You, Holy Spirit. I praise You, Holy Spirit. I worship You, Holy Spirit.
Amen.

> For we are his handiwork, created in
> Christ Jesus for the good works
> that God has prepared in advance,
> that we should live in them.
> Ephesians 2:10

Day 58

Before Father God I decree, and I declare in the name of Jesus Christ of Nazareth, that you, *my baby*, have access to God through the Spirit.

Thank You, Father. I praise You, Father. I worship You, Father. Thank You, Jesus. I praise You, Jesus. I worship You, Jesus. Thank You, Holy Spirit. I praise You, Holy Spirit. I worship You, Holy Spirit.
Amen.

> For through him we both have access
> in one Spirit to the Father.
> Ephesians 2:18

Day 59

Before Father God I decree, and I declare in the name of Jesus Christ of Nazareth, that you, *my baby*, are a citizen of God's family.

Thank You, Father. I praise You, Father. I worship You, Father. Thank You, Jesus. I praise You, Jesus. I worship You, Jesus. Thank You, Holy Spirit. I praise You, Holy Spirit. I worship You, Holy Spirit.
Amen.

So then you are no longer strangers and
sojourners, but you are fellow citizens
with the holy ones and members of the household of God.
Ephesians 2:19

Day 60

Before Father God I decree, and I declare in the name of Jesus Christ of Nazareth, that you, *my baby*, belong to the household of God, built upon the foundation of the apostles and prophets, with Christ Jesus himself as the capstone.

Thank You, Father. I praise You, Father. I worship You, Father. Thank You, Jesus. I praise You, Jesus. I worship You, Jesus. Thank You, Holy Spirit. I praise You, Holy Spirit. I worship You, Holy Spirit.
Amen.

The household of God [is] built upon the
foundation of the apostles and prophets,
with Christ Jesus himself as the capstone.
Ephesians 2:19–20

Day 61

Before Father God I decree, and I declare in the name of Jesus Christ of Nazareth, that you, *my baby*, are being built together with Jesus Christ into a dwelling place of God in the Spirit.

Thank You, Father. I praise You, Father. I worship You, Father. Thank You, Jesus. I praise You, Jesus. I worship You, Jesus. Thank You, Holy Spirit. I praise You, Holy Spirit. I worship You, Holy Spirit.
Amen.

In him you are also are being built together
into a dwelling place of God in the Spirit.
Ephesians 2:22

Day 62

Before Father God I decree, and I declare in the name of Jesus Christ of Nazareth, that you, *my baby*, know God's mysteries by revelation.

Thank You, Father. I praise You, Father. I worship You, Father. Thank You, Jesus. I praise You, Jesus. I worship You, Jesus. Thank You, Holy Spirit. I praise You, Holy Spirit. I worship You, Holy Spirit.
Amen.

The mystery was made known to me by revelation.
Ephesians 3:3

Day 63

Before Father God I decree, and I declare in the name of Jesus Christ of Nazareth, that you, *my baby*, are strengthened in the inner self with power through God's Spirit.

Thank You, Father. I praise You, Father. I worship You, Father. Thank You, Jesus. I praise You, Jesus. I worship You, Jesus. Thank You, Holy Spirit. I praise You, Holy Spirit. I worship You, Holy Spirit.
Amen.

> That he may grant you in accord with the
> riches of his glory to be strengthened
> with power through his Spirit in the inner self.
> Ephesians 3:16

Day 64

Before Father God I decree, and I declare in the name of Jesus Christ of Nazareth, that you, *my baby*, belong to Christ. Christ dwells in your heart through faith. You have been rooted and grounded in love.

Thank You, Father. I praise You, Father. I worship You, Father. Thank You, Jesus. I praise You, Jesus. I worship You, Jesus. Thank You, Holy Spirit. I praise You, Holy Spirit. I worship You, Holy Spirit.
Amen.

> And that Christ may dwell in your hearts through
> faith, that you, rooted and grounded in love,
> may have strength to comprehend with all the holy ones
> what is the breadth and length and height and depth.
> Ephesians 3:17–18

Day 65

Before Father God I decree, and I declare in the name of Jesus Christ of Nazareth, that you, *my baby*, know the love of Christ that surpasses knowledge. You have been filled with all the fullness of God.

Thank You, Father. I praise You, Father. I worship You, Father. Thank You, Jesus. I praise You, Jesus. I worship You, Jesus. Thank You, Holy Spirit. I praise You, Holy Spirit. I worship You, Holy Spirit.
Amen.

And to know the love of Christ that surpasses knowledge,
so that you may be filled with all the fullness of God.
Ephesians 3:19

Day 66

Before Father God I decree, and I declare in the name of Jesus Christ of Nazareth, that you, *my baby*, can accomplish far more than all we ask or imagine by the power at work within you.

Thank You, Father. I praise You, Father. I worship You, Father. Thank You, Jesus. I praise You, Jesus. I worship You, Jesus. Thank You, Holy Spirit. I praise You, Holy Spirit. I worship You, Holy Spirit.
Amen.

Now to him who is able to accomplish far
more than all we ask or imagine,
by the power at work within us.
Ephesians 3:20

Day 67

Before Father God I decree, and I declare in the name of Jesus Christ of Nazareth, that you, *my baby*, have received grace according to the measure of Christ's gift.

Thank You, Father. I praise You, Father. I worship You, Father. Thank You, Jesus. I praise You, Jesus. I worship You, Jesus. Thank You, Holy Spirit. I praise You, Holy Spirit. I worship You, Holy Spirit.
Amen.

> But grace was given to each of us according
> to the measure of Christ's gift.
> Ephesians 4:7

Day 68

Before Father God I decree, and I declare in the name of Jesus Christ of Nazareth, that you, *my baby*, will live the truth in love. You will grow in every way into Him who is the head, Christ.

Thank You, Father. I praise You, Father. I worship You, Father. Thank You, Jesus. I praise You, Jesus. I worship You, Jesus. Thank You, Holy Spirit. I praise You, Holy Spirit. I worship You, Holy Spirit.
Amen.

> Rather, living the truth in love, we should grow in
> every way into him who is the head, Christ.
> Ephesians 4:15

Day 69

Before Father God I decree, and I declare in the name of Jesus Christ of Nazareth, that you, *my baby*, have been renewed in the Spirit of your mind.

Thank You, Father. I praise You, Father. I worship You, Father. Thank You, Jesus. I praise You, Jesus. I worship You, Jesus. Thank You, Holy Spirit. I praise You, Holy Spirit. I worship You, Holy Spirit.
Amen.

> And be renewed in the spirit of your minds.
> Ephesians 4:23

Day 70

Before Father God I decree, and I declare in the name of Jesus Christ of Nazareth, that you, *my baby*, will speak only good words, such as are needed for edification, that your words will impart grace to those who hear.

Thank You, Father. I praise You, Father. I worship You, Father. Thank You, Jesus. I praise You, Jesus. I worship You, Jesus. Thank You, Holy Spirit. I praise You, Holy Spirit. I worship You, Holy Spirit.
Amen.

> No foul language should come out of your mouths,
> but only such as is good for needed edification,
> that it may impart grace to those who hear.
> Ephesians 4:29

Day 71

Before Father God I decree, and I declare in the name of Jesus Christ of Nazareth, that you, *my baby*, will not grieve the Holy Spirit of God with which you are sealed for the day of redemption.

Thank You, Father. I praise You, Father. I worship You, Father.
Thank You, Jesus. I praise You, Jesus. I worship You, Jesus.
Thank You, Holy Spirit. I praise You, Holy Spirit. I worship You, Holy Spirit.
Amen.

> And do not grieve the holy Spirit of God with which
> you are sealed for the day of redemption.
> Ephesians 4:30

Day 72

Before Father God I decree, and I declare in the name of Jesus Christ of Nazareth, that you, *my baby*, are an imitator of God as a beloved child. You live in love as Christ loved you and handed Himself over for you as a sacrificial offering to God for a fragrant aroma.

Thank You, Father. I praise You, Father. I worship You, Father.
Thank You, Jesus. I praise You, Jesus. I worship You, Jesus.
Thank You, Holy Spirit. I praise You, Holy Spirit. I worship You, Holy Spirit.
Amen.

> So be imitators of God, as beloved children, and live in love,
> as Christ loved us and handed himself over for us
> as a sacrificial offering to God for a fragrant aroma.
> Ephesians 5:1–2

Day 73

Before Father God I decree, and I declare in the name of Jesus Christ of Nazareth, that you, *my baby*, are light in the Lord.

Thank You, Father. I praise You, Father. I worship You, Father. Thank You, Jesus. I praise You, Jesus. I worship You, Jesus. Thank You, Holy Spirit. I praise You, Holy Spirit. I worship You, Holy Spirit.
Amen.

> For you were once darkness but now you are
> light in the Lord. Live as children of light.
> Ephesians 5:8

Day 74

Before Father God I decree, and I declare in the name of Jesus Christ of Nazareth, that you, *my baby*, are wise. You will make the most of the opportunity.

Thank You, Father. I praise You, Father. I worship You, Father. Thank You, Jesus. I praise You, Jesus. I worship You, Jesus. Thank You, Holy Spirit. I praise You, Holy Spirit. I worship You, Holy Spirit.
Amen.

> Watch carefully then how you live, not
> as foolish person but as wise,
> making the most of the opportunity,
> because the days are evil.
> Ephesians 5:15–16

Day 75

Before Father God I decree, and I declare in the name of Jesus Christ of Nazareth, that you, *my baby*, are singing and playing to the Lord in your heart. You are always giving thanks for everything in the name of the Lord Jesus Christ to God the Father.

Thank You, Father. I praise You, Father. I worship You, Father. Thank You, Jesus. I praise You, Jesus. I worship You, Jesus. Thank You, Holy Spirit. I praise You, Holy Spirit. I worship You, Holy Spirit.
Amen.

Addressing one another in psalms and
hymns and spiritual songs,
singing and playing to the Lord in your hearts,
giving thanks always and for everything
in the name of our Lord Jesus Christ to God the Father.
Ephesians 5:19–20

Day 76

Before Father God I decree, and I declare in the name of Jesus Christ of Nazareth, that you, *my baby*, are willingly serving the Lord, knowing that each will be requited from the Lord for whatever good you do.

Thank You, Father. I praise You, Father. I worship You, Father. Thank You, Jesus. I praise You, Jesus. I worship You, Jesus. Thank You, Holy Spirit. I praise You, Holy Spirit. I worship You, Holy Spirit.
Amen.

Willingly serv[e] the Lord and not human beings,
knowing that each will be requited from the Lord
for whatever good he does, whether he is slave or free.
Ephesians 6:7–8

Day 77

Before Father God I decree, and I declare in the name of Jesus Christ of Nazareth, that you, *my baby*, have been drawing your strength from the Lord and from His mighty power.

Thank You, Father. I praise You, Father. I worship You, Father. Thank You, Jesus. I praise You, Jesus. I worship You, Jesus. Thank You, Holy Spirit. I praise You, Holy Spirit. I worship You, Holy Spirit.
Amen.

> Finally, draw your strength from the
> Lord and from his mighty power.
> Ephesians 6:10

Day 78

Before Father God I decree, and I declare in the name of Jesus Christ of Nazareth, that you, *my baby*, are dressed in the armor of God. You are always standing firm against the tactics of the devil.

Thank You, Father. I praise You, Father. I worship You, Father. Thank You, Jesus. I praise You, Jesus. I worship You, Jesus. Thank You, Holy Spirit. I praise You, Holy Spirit. I worship You, Holy Spirit.
Amen.

> Put on the armor of God so that you may be able
> to stand firm against the tactics of the devil.
> Ephesians 6:11

Day 79

Before Father God I decree, and I declare in the name of Jesus Christ of Nazareth, that you, *my baby*, have received the sword of the Spirit, which is the Word of God.

Thank You, Father. I praise You, Father. I worship You, Father. Thank You, Jesus. I praise You, Jesus. I worship You, Jesus. Thank You, Holy Spirit. I praise You, Holy Spirit. I worship You, Holy Spirit.
Amen.

> And take the helmet of salvation and sword
> of the Spirit, which is the word of God.
> Ephesians 6:17

Day 80

Before Father God I decree, and I declare in the name of Jesus Christ of Nazareth, that you, *my baby*, are clothed with righteousness as a breastplate.

Thank You, Father. I praise You, Father. I worship You, Father. Thank You, Jesus. I praise You, Jesus. I worship You, Jesus. Thank You, Holy Spirit. I praise You, Holy Spirit. I worship You, Holy Spirit.
Amen.

> So, stand fast with your loins girded in truth,
> clothed with righteousness as a breastplate.
> Ephesians 6:14

Day 81

Before Father God I decree, and I declare in the name of Jesus Christ of Nazareth, that you, my baby, will not fall short in speech. You are a perfect child, able to bridle your whole body also.

Thank You, Father. I praise You, Father. I worship You, Father. Thank You, Jesus. I praise You, Jesus. I worship You, Jesus. Thank You, Holy Spirit. I praise You, Holy Spirit. I worship You, Holy Spirit.
Amen.

> For we all fall short in many respects. If
> anyone does not fall short in speech,
> he is a perfect man, able to bridle his whole body also.
> James 3:2

Day 82

Before Father God I decree, and I declare in the name of Jesus Christ of Nazareth, that you, *my baby*, have been given all power in heaven and on the earth through Jesus.

Thank You, Father. I praise You, Father. I worship You, Father. Thank You, Jesus. I praise You, Jesus. I worship You, Jesus. Thank You, Holy Spirit. I praise You, Holy Spirit. I worship You, Holy Spirit.
Amen.

> Then Jesus approached and said to them,
> "All power in heaven and on the earth
> has been given to me."
> Matthew 28:18

Day 83

Before Father God I decree, and I declare in the name of Jesus Christ of Nazareth, that you, *my baby*, are commanded to make disciples.

Thank You, Father. I praise You, Father. I worship You, Father.
Thank You, Jesus. I praise You, Jesus. I worship You, Jesus.
Thank You, Holy Spirit. I praise You, Holy Spirit. I worship You, Holy Spirit.
Amen.

Make disciples of all nations ... teaching them
to observe all that I have commanded you.
And behold, I am with you always, until the end of the age.
Matthew 28:19–20

Day 84

Before Father God I decree, and I declare in the name of Jesus Christ of Nazareth, that you, *my baby*, are always with Jesus until the end of the age.

Thank You, Father. I praise You, Father. I worship You, Father.
Thank You, Jesus. I praise You, Jesus. I worship You, Jesus.
Thank You, Holy Spirit. I praise You, Holy Spirit. I worship You, Holy Spirit.
Amen.

Teaching them to observe all that I have commanded you.
And behold, I am with you always, until the end of the age.
Matthew 28:20

Day 85

Before Father God I decree, and I declare in the name of Jesus Christ of Nazareth, that you, *my baby*, are a child of God.

Thank You, Father. I praise You, Father. I worship You, Father. Thank You, Jesus. I praise You, Jesus. I worship You, Jesus. Thank You, Holy Spirit. I praise You, Holy Spirit. I worship You, Holy Spirit.
Amen.

> But to those who did accept him he gave
> power to become children of God,
> to those who believe in his name.
> John 1:12

Day 86

Before Father God I decree, and I declare in the name of Jesus Christ of Nazareth, that you, *my baby*, were born not by human choice nor by man's decision but of God.

Thank You, Father. I praise You, Father. I worship You, Father. Thank You, Jesus. I praise You, Jesus. I worship You, Jesus. Thank You, Holy Spirit. I praise You, Holy Spirit. I worship You, Holy Spirit.
Amen.

> Who were born not by natural generation
> nor by human choice
> nor by man's decision but of God.
> John 1:13

Day 87

Before Father God I decree, and I declare in the name of Jesus Christ of Nazareth, that you, *my baby*, have been given peace.

Thank You, Father. I praise You, Father. I worship You, Father. Thank You, Jesus. I praise You, Jesus. I worship You, Jesus. Thank You, Holy Spirit. I praise You, Holy Spirit. I worship You, Holy Spirit.
Amen.

> Peace I leave with you; my peace I give to you.
> John 14:27

Day 88

Before Father God I decree, and I declare in the name of Jesus Christ of Nazareth, that you, *my baby*, have eternal life.

Thank You, Father. I praise You, Father. I worship You, Father. Thank You, Jesus. I praise You, Jesus. I worship You, Jesus. Thank You, Holy Spirit. I praise You, Holy Spirit. I worship You, Holy Spirit.
Amen.

> I give them eternal life, and they shall never perish.
> No one can take them out of my hand.
> John 10:28

Day 89

Before Father God I decree, and I declare in the name of Jesus Christ of Nazareth, that you, *my baby*, hear God's voice. God knows you, and you follow Him.

Thank You, Father. I praise You, Father. I worship You, Father. Thank You, Jesus. I praise You, Jesus. I worship You, Jesus. Thank You, Holy Spirit. I praise You, Holy Spirit. I worship You, Holy Spirit.
Amen.

My sheep hear my voice; I know them, and they follow me.
John 10:27

Day 90

Before Father God I decree, and I declare in the name of Jesus Christ of Nazareth, that you, *my baby*, are part of the true vine. You will bear fruit in everything you do.

Thank You, Father. I praise You, Father. I worship You, Father. Thank You, Jesus. I praise You, Jesus. I worship You, Jesus. Thank You, Holy Spirit. I praise You, Holy Spirit. I worship You, Holy Spirit.
Amen.

I am the true vine, and my Father is vine grower ...
Whoever remains in me and I in him will bear much fruit,
because without me you can do nothing.
John 15: 1, 5

Day 91

Before Father God I decree, and I declare in the name of Jesus Christ of Nazareth, that you, *my baby*, are pruned.

Thank You, Father. I praise You, Father. I worship You, Father. Thank You, Jesus. I praise You, Jesus. I worship You, Jesus. Thank You, Holy Spirit. I praise You, Holy Spirit. I worship You, Holy Spirit.
Amen.

> You are already pruned because of
> the word that I spoke to you.
> John 15:3

Day 92

Before Father God I decree, and I declare in the name of Jesus Christ of Nazareth, that you, *my baby*, are Christ's friend.

Thank You, Father. I praise You, Father. I worship You, Father. Thank You, Jesus. I praise You, Jesus. I worship You, Jesus. Thank You, Holy Spirit. I praise You, Holy Spirit. I worship You, Holy Spirit.
Amen.

> I no longer call you slaves, because a slave does not know
> what his master doing. I have called you friends,
> because I told you everything I have heard from my Father.
> John 15:15

Day 93

Before Father God I decree, and I declare in the name of Jesus Christ of Nazareth, that you, *my baby*, are chosen and appointed by Christ to bear His fruit.

Thank You, Father. I praise You, Father. I worship You, Father. Thank You, Jesus. I praise You, Jesus. I worship You, Jesus. Thank You, Holy Spirit. I praise You, Holy Spirit. I worship You, Holy Spirit.
Amen.

It was not you who chose me, but I who chose you
and appointed you to go and bear fruit that will remain,
John 15:16

Day 94

Before Father God I decree, and I declare in the name of Jesus Christ of Nazareth, that you, *my baby*, will receive whatever you ask the Father in Jesus's name.

Thank You, Father. I praise You, Father. I worship You, Father. Thank You, Jesus. I praise You, Jesus. I worship You, Jesus. Thank You, Holy Spirit. I praise You, Holy Spirit. I worship You, Holy Spirit.
Amen.

Whatever you ask the Father in my name he may give you.
John 15:16

Day 95

Before Father God I decree, and I declare in the name of Jesus Christ of Nazareth, that you, *my baby*, will be guided to all truth by the Spirit of truth. The Spirit of truth will declare to you the things that are coming.

Thank You, Father. I praise You, Father. I worship You, Father. Thank You, Jesus. I praise You, Jesus. I worship You, Jesus. Thank You, Holy Spirit. I praise You, Holy Spirit. I worship You, Holy Spirit.
Amen.

> But when he comes, the Spirit of truth,
> he will guide you to all truth.
> He will not speak on his own, but he
> will speak what he hears,
> and will declare to you the things that are coming.
> John 16:13

Day 96

Before Father God I decree, and I declare in the name of Jesus Christ of Nazareth, that you, *my baby*, have received everything what the Father has.

Thank You, Father. I praise You, Father. I worship You, Father. Thank You, Jesus. I praise You, Jesus. I worship You, Jesus. Thank You, Holy Spirit. I praise You, Holy Spirit. I worship You, Holy Spirit.
Amen.

> Everything that the Father has is mine; for
> this reason I told you that he will take from
> what is mine and declare it to you.
> John 16:15

Day 97

Before Father God I decree, and I declare in the name of Jesus Christ of Nazareth, that you, *my baby*, have been justified, completely forgiven, and made righteous.

Thank You, Father. I praise You, Father. I worship You, Father. Thank You, Jesus. I praise You, Jesus. I worship You, Jesus. Thank You, Holy Spirit. I praise You, Holy Spirit. I worship You, Holy Spirit.
Amen.

Therefore, since we have been justified by faith,
we have peace with God through our Lord Jesus Christ.
Romans 5:1

Day 98

Before Father God I decree, and I declare in the name of Jesus Christ of Nazareth, that you, *my baby*, are free from sin and have become a slave of righteousness.

Thank You, Father. I praise You, Father. I worship You, Father. Thank You, Jesus. I praise You, Jesus. I worship You, Jesus. Thank You, Holy Spirit. I praise You, Holy Spirit. I worship You, Holy Spirit.
Amen.

Freed from sin, you have become slaves of righteousness.
Romans 6:18

Day 99

Before Father God I decree, and I declare in the name of Jesus Christ of Nazareth, that you, *my baby*, are free from sin and enslaved to God.

Thank You, Father. I praise You, Father. I worship You, Father. Thank You, Jesus. I praise You, Jesus. I worship You, Jesus. Thank You, Holy Spirit. I praise You, Holy Spirit. I worship You, Holy Spirit.
Amen.

> But now that you have been free from sin
> and have become slaves of God,
> the benefit that you have leads to
> sanctification and its end is eternal life.
> Romans 6:22

Day 100

Before Father God I decree, and I declare in the name of Jesus Christ of Nazareth, that you, *my baby*, are free forever from condemnation.

Thank You, Father. I praise You, Father. I worship You, Father. Thank You, Jesus. I praise You, Jesus. I worship You, Jesus. Thank You, Holy Spirit. I praise You, Holy Spirit. I worship You, Holy Spirit.
Amen.

> Hence, now there is no condemnation
> for those who are in Christ Jesus.
> Romans 8:1

Day 101

Before Father God I decree, and I declare in the name of Jesus Christ of Nazareth, that you, *my baby*, are not in flesh. You are in the Spirit; the Spirit of God dwells in you.

Thank You, Father. I praise You, Father. I worship You, Father. Thank You, Jesus. I praise You, Jesus. I worship You, Jesus. Thank You, Holy Spirit. I praise You, Holy Spirit. I worship You, Holy Spirit.
Amen.

> But you are not in flesh; on the
> contrary, you are in the spirit,
> if only the Spirit of God dwells in you.
> Romans 8:9

Day 102

Before Father God I decree, and I declare in the name of Jesus Christ of Nazareth, that you, *my baby*, are a child of God. God is your spiritual Father; you will call God *Abba*, Father.

Thank You, Father. I praise You, Father. I worship You, Father. Thank You, Jesus. I praise You, Jesus. I worship You, Jesus. Thank You, Holy Spirit. I praise You, Holy Spirit. I worship You, Holy Spirit.
Amen.

> For those who are led by the Spirit of
> God are children of God …
> you received a spirit of adoption, through
> which we cry, "Abba, Father!"
> Romans 8:14–15

Day 103

Before Father God I decree, and I declare in the name of Jesus Christ of Nazareth, that you, *my baby*, are a joint heir with Christ. You are sharing God's inheritance with Christ.

Thank You, Father. I praise You, Father. I worship You, Father. Thank You, Jesus. I praise You, Jesus. I worship You, Jesus. Thank You, Holy Spirit. I praise You, Holy Spirit. I worship You, Holy Spirit.
Amen.

> We are children of God, and if children, then
> heirs, heirs of God and joint heirs with Christ,
> if only we suffer with him so that we
> may also be glorified with him.
> Romans 8:16–17

Day 104

Before Father God I decree, and I declare in the name of Jesus Christ of Nazareth, that you, *my baby*, were saved in hope.

Thank You, Father. I praise You, Father. I worship You, Father. Thank You, Jesus. I praise You, Jesus. I worship You, Jesus. Thank You, Holy Spirit. I praise You, Holy Spirit. I worship You, Holy Spirit.
Amen.

> For in hope we were saved. Now hope
> that sees for itself is not hope.
> For who hopes for what one sees?
> Romans 8:24

Day 105

Before Father God I decree, and I declare in the name of Jesus Christ of Nazareth, that you, *my baby*, have hope for what you do not see, and you wait with endurance.

Thank You, Father. I praise You, Father. I worship You, Father. Thank You, Jesus. I praise You, Jesus. I worship You, Jesus. Thank You, Holy Spirit. I praise You, Holy Spirit. I worship You, Holy Spirit.
Amen.

Romans 8:25
But if we hope for what we do not
see, we wait with endurance.

Day 106

Before Father God I decree, and I declare in the name of Jesus Christ of Nazareth, that you, my baby, are more than a conqueror through Christ, who loves you.

Thank You, Father. I praise You, Father. I worship You, Father. Thank You, Jesus. I praise You, Jesus. I worship You, Jesus. Thank You, Holy Spirit. I praise You, Holy Spirit. I worship You, Holy Spirit.
Amen.

Romans 8:37
No, in all these things we conquer
overwhelmingly through him who loved us.

Day 107

Before Father God I decree, and I declare in the name of Jesus Christ of Nazareth, that you, *my baby*, have the measure of faith to think clearly.

Thank You, Father. I praise You, Father. I worship You, Father. Thank You, Jesus. I praise You, Jesus. I worship You, Jesus. Thank You, Holy Spirit. I praise You, Holy Spirit. I worship You, Holy Spirit.
Amen.

> For by the grace given to me I tell everyone among you … to think soberly, each according to the measure of faith that God has apportioned.
> Romans 12:3

Day 108

Before Father God I decree, and I declare in the name of Jesus Christ of Nazareth, that you, *my baby*, have been sanctified and called to holiness.

Thank You, Father. I praise You, Father. I worship You, Father. Thank You, Jesus. I praise You, Jesus. I worship You, Jesus. Thank You, Holy Spirit. I praise You, Holy Spirit. I worship You, Holy Spirit.
Amen.

> You … have been sanctified in Christ Jesus, called to be holy.
> 1 Corinthians 1:2

Day 109

Before Father God I decree, and I declare in the name of Jesus Christ of Nazareth, that you, *my baby*, have been given grace in Christ Jesus.

Thank You, Father. I praise You, Father. I worship You, Father. Thank You, Jesus. I praise You, Jesus. I worship You, Jesus. Thank You, Holy Spirit. I praise You, Holy Spirit. I worship You, Holy Spirit.
Amen.

I give thanks to my God always on your account
for the grace of God bestowed on you in Christ Jesus.
1 Corinthians 1:4

Day 110

Before Father God I decree, and I declare in the name of Jesus Christ of Nazareth, that you, *my baby*, were enriched in Christ in every way, with all discourse and all knowledge.

Thank You, Father. I praise You, Father. I worship You, Father. Thank You, Jesus. I praise You, Jesus. I worship You, Jesus. Thank You, Holy Spirit. I praise You, Holy Spirit. I worship You, Holy Spirit.
Amen.

That in him you were enriched in every way,
with all discourse and all knowledge.
1 Corinthians 1:5

Day 111

Before Father God I decree, and I declare in the name of Jesus Christ of Nazareth, that you, *my baby*, are not lacking any spiritual gift.

Thank You, Father. I praise You, Father. I worship You, Father. Thank You, Jesus. I praise You, Jesus. I worship You, Jesus. Thank You, Holy Spirit. I praise You, Holy Spirit. I worship You, Holy Spirit.
Amen.

So that you are not lacking in any spiritual gift
as you wait for the revelation of our Lord Jesus Christ.
1 Corinthians 1:7

Day 112

Before Father God I decree, and I declare in the name of Jesus Christ of Nazareth, that you, *my baby*, were called by God to fellowship with His Son, Jesus Christ.

Thank You, Father. I praise You, Father. I worship You, Father. Thank You, Jesus. I praise You, Jesus. I worship You, Jesus. Thank You, Holy Spirit. I praise You, Holy Spirit. I worship You, Holy Spirit.
Amen.

God is faithful, and by Him you were called to
fellowship with his Son, Jesus Christ our Lord.
1 Corinthians 1:9

Day 113

Before Father God I decree, and I declare in the name of Jesus Christ of Nazareth, that you, *my baby*, have been placed into Christ, by God's doing.

Thank You, Father. I praise You, Father. I worship You, Father. Thank You, Jesus. I praise You, Jesus. I worship You, Jesus. Thank You, Holy Spirit. I praise You, Holy Spirit. I worship You, Holy Spirit.
Amen.

> It is due to him that you are in Christ Jesus.
> Corinthians 1:30

Day 114

Before Father God I decree, and I declare in the name of Jesus Christ of Nazareth, that you, *my baby*, have received the Spirit from God, so that you may understand the things freely given to you by God.

Thank You, Father. I praise You, Father. I worship You, Father. Thank You, Jesus. I praise You, Jesus. I worship You, Jesus. Thank You, Holy Spirit. I praise You, Holy Spirit. I worship You, Holy Spirit.
Amen.

> We have not received that spirit of the
> world but the Spirit that is from God,
> so that we may understand the things
> freely given us by God.
> 1 Corinthians 2:12

Day 115

Before Father God I decree, and I declare in the name of Jesus Christ of Nazareth, that you, *my baby,* have the mind of Christ.

Thank You, Father. I praise You, Father. I worship You, Father. Thank You, Jesus. I praise You, Jesus. I worship You, Jesus. Thank You, Holy Spirit. I praise You, Holy Spirit. I worship You, Holy Spirit.
Amen.

But we have the mind of Christ.
1 Corinthians 2:16

Day 116

Before Father God I decree, and I declare in the name of Jesus Christ of Nazareth, that you, *my baby*, are the temple of God. His Spirit, His life, dwells in you.

Thank You, Father. I praise You, Father. I worship You, Father. Thank You, Jesus. I praise You, Jesus. I worship You, Jesus. Thank You, Holy Spirit. I praise You, Holy Spirit. I worship You, Holy Spirit.
Amen.

Do you know that you are the temple of God,
and that the Spirit of God dwells in you?
1 Corinthians 3:16

Day 117

Before Father God I decree, and I declare in the name of Jesus Christ of Nazareth, that you, *my baby*, are united to the Lord and are one spirit with Him.

Thank You, Father. I praise You, Father. I worship You, Father. Thank You, Jesus. I praise You, Jesus. I worship You, Jesus. Thank You, Holy Spirit. I praise You, Holy Spirit. I worship You, Holy Spirit.
Amen.

> But whoever is joined to the Lord
> becomes one spirit with him.
> 1 Corinthians 6:17

Day 118

Before Father God I decree, and I declare in the name of Jesus Christ of Nazareth, that you, *my baby*, have been purchased at a price.

Thank You, Father. I praise You, Father. I worship You, Father. Thank You, Jesus. I praise You, Jesus. I worship You, Jesus. Thank You, Holy Spirit. I praise You, Holy Spirit. I worship You, Holy Spirit.
Amen.

> For you have been purchased at a price.
> Therefore, glorify God in your body.
> 1 Corinthians 6:20

Day 119

Before Father God I decree, and I declare in the name of Jesus Christ of Nazareth, that you, *my baby*, are called by God.

Thank You, Father. I praise You, Father. I worship You, Father. Thank You, Jesus. I praise You, Jesus. I worship You, Jesus. Thank You, Holy Spirit. I praise You, Holy Spirit. I worship You, Holy Spirit.
Amen.

Just as God called each one.
1 Corinthians 7:17

Day 120

Before Father God I decree, and I declare in the name of Jesus Christ of Nazareth, that you, *my baby,* are a member of Christ's body.

Thank You, Father. I praise You, Father. I worship You, Father. Thank You, Jesus. I praise You, Jesus. I worship You, Jesus. Thank You, Holy Spirit. I praise You, Holy Spirit. I worship You, Holy Spirit.
Amen.

Now you are Christ's body, and individually parts of it.
1 Corinthians 12:27

Day 121

Before Father God I decree, and I declare in the name of Jesus Christ of Nazareth, that you, *my baby*, are victorious through Jesus Christ.

Thank You, Father. I praise You, Father. I worship You, Father. Thank You, Jesus. I praise You, Jesus. I worship You, Jesus. Thank You, Holy Spirit. I praise You, Holy Spirit. I worship You, Holy Spirit.
Amen.

> But thanks be to God who give us the
> victory through our Lord Jesus Christ.
> 1 Corinthians 15:57

Day 122

Before Father God I decree, and I declare in the name of Jesus Christ of Nazareth, that you, *my baby*, are led by God in triumph in Christ.

Thank You, Father. I praise You, Father. I worship You, Father. Thank You, Jesus. I praise You, Jesus. I worship You, Jesus. Thank You, Holy Spirit. I praise You, Holy Spirit. I worship You, Holy Spirit.
Amen.

> But thanks be to God, who always
> leads us in triumph in Christ.
> 2 Corinthians 2:14

Day 123

Before Father God I decree, and I declare in the name of Jesus Christ of Nazareth, that you, *my baby*, are the fragrance of Christ for God.

Thank You, Father. I praise You, Father. I worship You, Father. Thank You, Jesus. I praise You, Jesus. I worship You, Jesus. Thank You, Holy Spirit. I praise You, Holy Spirit. I worship You, Holy Spirit.
Amen.

> For we are the aroma of Christ for God
> among those who are being saved
> and among those who are perishing.
> 2 Corinthians 2:15

Day 124

Before Father God I decree, and I declare in the name of Jesus Christ of Nazareth, that you, *my baby*, are a child of God in Christ Jesus.

Thank You, Father. I praise You, Father. I worship You, Father. Thank You, Jesus. I praise You, Jesus. I worship You, Jesus. Thank You, Holy Spirit. I praise You, Holy Spirit. I worship You, Holy Spirit.
Amen.

> For through faith you are all children of God in Christ Jesus.
> Galatians 3:26

Day 125

Before Father God I decree, and I declare in the name of Jesus Christ of Nazareth, that you, *my baby*, are Abraham's descendant.

Thank You, Father. I praise You, Father. I worship You, Father. Thank You, Jesus. I praise You, Jesus. I worship You, Jesus. Thank You, Holy Spirit. I praise You, Holy Spirit. I worship You, Holy Spirit.
Amen.

> And if you belong to Christ, then you
> are Abraham's descendant,
> heirs according to the promise.
> Galatians 3:29

Day 126

Before Father God I decree, and I declare in the name of Jesus Christ of Nazareth, that you, *my baby*, have been transferred to the kingdom of Christ.

Thank You, Father. I praise You, Father. I worship You, Father. Thank You, Jesus. I praise You, Jesus. I worship You, Jesus. Thank You, Holy Spirit. I praise You, Holy Spirit. I worship You, Holy Spirit.
Amen.

> And transferred us to the kingdom of his beloved Son.
> Colossians 1:13

Day 127

Before Father God I decree, and I declare in the name of Jesus Christ of Nazareth, that you, *my baby*, are blameless and free from accusation.

Thank You, Father. I praise You, Father. I worship You, Father. Thank You, Jesus. I praise You, Jesus. I worship You, Jesus. Thank You, Holy Spirit. I praise You, Holy Spirit. I worship You, Holy Spirit.
Amen.

He has now reconciled in his fleshly body
through his death, to present you holy,
without blemish, and irreproachable before him.
Colossians 1:22

Day 128

Before Father God I decree, and I declare in the name of Jesus Christ of Nazareth, that you, *my baby*, are firmly rooted in Christ. You are now being built up in Him.

Thank You, Father. I praise You, Father. I worship You, Father. Thank You, Jesus. I praise You, Jesus. I worship You, Jesus. Thank You, Holy Spirit. I praise You, Holy Spirit. I worship You, Holy Spirit.
Amen.

Walk in him, rooted in him and built upon him
and established in faith as you were
taught, abounding in thanksgiving.
Colossians 2:6–7

Day 129

Before Father God I decree, and I declare in the name of Jesus Christ of Nazareth, that you, *my baby*, have been made complete in Christ.

Thank You, Father. I praise You, Father. I worship You, Father. Thank You, Jesus. I praise You, Jesus. I worship You, Jesus. Thank You, Holy Spirit. I praise You, Holy Spirit. I worship You, Holy Spirit.
Amen.

> And you share in this fullness in him, who is
> the head of every principality and power.
> Colossians 2:10

Day 130

Before Father God I decree, and I declare in the name of Jesus Christ of Nazareth, that you, *my baby*, are an expression of the life of Christ, because He is your life.

Thank You, Father. I praise You, Father. I worship You, Father. Thank You, Jesus. I praise You, Jesus. I worship You, Jesus. Thank You, Holy Spirit. I praise You, Holy Spirit. I worship You, Holy Spirit.
Amen.

> When Christ your life appears, then you
> too will appear with him in glory.
> Colossians 3:4

Day 131

Before Father God I decree, and I declare in the name of Jesus Christ of Nazareth, that you, *my baby*, are chosen by God, holy and dearly loved. You are covered with compassion, kindness, humility, gentleness, and patience.

Thank You, Father. I praise You, Father. I worship You, Father. Thank You, Jesus. I praise You, Jesus. I worship You, Jesus. Thank You, Holy Spirit. I praise You, Holy Spirit. I worship You, Holy Spirit.
Amen.

> Put on then, as God's chosen ones, holy and beloved,
> heartfelt compassion, kindness, humility,
> gentleness, and patience.
> Colossians 3:12

Day 132

Before Father God I decree, and I declare in the name of Jesus Christ of Nazareth, that you, *my baby*, will let the Word of Christ dwell in you richly. In all wisdom you will teach.

Thank You, Father. I praise You, Father. I worship You, Father. Thank You, Jesus. I praise You, Jesus. I worship You, Jesus. Thank You, Holy Spirit. I praise You, Holy Spirit. I worship You, Holy Spirit.
Amen.

> Let the word of Christ dwell in you richly, as in all
> wisdom you teach and admonish one another,
> singing psalms, hymns, and spiritual songs
> with gratitude in your heats to God.
> Colossians 3:16

Day 133

Before Father God I decree, and I declare in the name of Jesus Christ of Nazareth, that you, *my baby*, will do everything in the name of the Lord Jesus.

Thank You, Father. I praise You, Father. I worship You, Father. Thank You, Jesus. I praise You, Jesus. I worship You, Jesus. Thank You, Holy Spirit. I praise You, Holy Spirit. I worship You, Holy Spirit.
Amen.

> And whatever you do, in word or in deed, do
> everything in the name of the Lord Jesus,
> giving thanks to God the Father through him.
> Colossians 3:17

Day 134

Before Father God I decree, and I declare in the name of Jesus Christ of Nazareth, that you, *my baby*, will obey your parents in everything, for this is pleasing to the Lord.

Thank You, Father. I praise You, Father. I worship You, Father. Thank You, Jesus. I praise You, Jesus. I worship You, Jesus. Thank You, Holy Spirit. I praise You, Holy Spirit. I worship You, Holy Spirit.
Amen.

> Children, obey your parents in everything,
> for this is pleasing to the Lord.
> Colossians 3:20

Day 135

Before Father God I decree, and I declare in the name of Jesus Christ of Nazareth, that you, *my baby*, will do everything from the heart, as for the Lord.

Thank You, Father. I praise You, Father. I worship You, Father. Thank You, Jesus. I praise You, Jesus. I worship You, Jesus. Thank You, Holy Spirit. I praise You, Holy Spirit. I worship You, Holy Spirit.
Amen.

> Whatever you do, do from the heart,
> as for the Lord not for others.
> Colossians 3:23

Day 136

Before Father God I decree, and I declare in the name of Jesus Christ of Nazareth, that you, *my baby*, will receive from the Lord the due payment of your inheritance.

Thank You, Father. I praise You, Father. I worship You, Father. Thank You, Jesus. I praise You, Jesus. I worship You, Jesus. Thank You, Holy Spirit. I praise You, Holy Spirit. I worship You, Holy Spirit.
Amen.

> Knowing that you will receive from the Lord
> the due payment of the inheritance,
> be slaves of the Lord Jesus Christ.
> Colossians 3:24

Day 137

Before Father God I decree, and I declare in the name of Jesus Christ of Nazareth, that you, *my baby*, will persevere in prayer, being watchful in it with thanksgiving.

Thank You, Father. I praise You, Father. I worship You, Father. Thank You, Jesus. I praise You, Jesus. I worship You, Jesus. Thank You, Holy Spirit. I praise You, Holy Spirit. I worship You, Holy Spirit.
Amen.

Persevere in prayer, being watchful in it with thanksgiving.
Colossians 4:2

Day 138

Before Father God I decree, and I declare in the name of Jesus Christ of Nazareth, that you, my baby, will conduct yourself wisely, making the most of opportunity.

Thank You, Father. I praise You, Father. I worship You, Father. Thank You, Jesus. I praise You, Jesus. I worship You, Jesus. Thank You, Holy Spirit. I praise You, Holy Spirit. I worship You, Holy Spirit.
Amen.

Conduct yourselves wisely toward outsiders,
making the most of the opportunity.
Colossians 4:5

Day 139

Before Father God I decree, and I declare in the name of Jesus Christ of Nazareth, that you, *my baby*, will let your speech always be gracious, seasoned with salt, so that you know how you should respond to each one.

Thank You, Father. I praise You, Father. I worship You, Father. Thank You, Jesus. I praise You, Jesus. I worship You, Jesus. Thank You, Holy Spirit. I praise You, Holy Spirit. I worship You, Holy Spirit.
Amen.

Let your speech always be gracious, seasoned with salt,
so that you know how you should respond to each one.
Colossians 4:6

Day 140

Before Father God I decree, and I declare in the name of Jesus Christ of Nazareth, that you, *my baby*, are Jesus's brother. Jesus is not ashamed to call you brother.

Thank You, Father. I praise You, Father. I worship You, Father. Thank You, Jesus. I praise You, Jesus. I worship You, Jesus. Thank You, Holy Spirit. I praise You, Holy Spirit. I worship You, Holy Spirit.
Amen.

He who consecrates and those who are
being consecrated all have one origin.
Therefore, he is not ashamed to call them "brothers."
Hebrews 2:11

Day 141

Before Father God I decree, and I declare in the name of Jesus Christ of Nazareth, that you, *my baby*, have received a heavenly calling.

Thank You, Father. I praise You, Father. I worship You, Father. Thank You, Jesus. I praise You, Jesus. I worship You, Jesus. Thank You, Holy Spirit. I praise You, Holy Spirit. I worship You, Holy Spirit.
Amen.

Therefore, holy "brothers," [share] in a heavenly calling.
Hebrews 3:1

Day 142

Before Father God I decree, and I declare in the name of Jesus Christ of Nazareth, that you, *my baby*, will always reflect on Jesus, the apostle and high priest of our confession.

Thank You, Father. I praise You, Father. I worship You, Father. Thank You, Jesus. I praise You, Jesus. I worship You, Jesus. Thank You, Holy Spirit. I praise You, Holy Spirit. I worship You, Holy Spirit.
Amen.

Therefore, holy "brothers," ... reflect on Jesus,
the apostle and high priest of our confession.
Hebrews 3:1

Day 143

Before Father God I decree, and I declare in the name of Jesus Christ of Nazareth, that you, *my baby*, are Jesus Christ's house.

Thank You, Father. I praise You, Father. I worship You, Father. Thank You, Jesus. I praise You, Jesus. I worship You, Jesus. Thank You, Holy Spirit. I praise You, Holy Spirit. I worship You, Holy Spirit.
Amen.

> But Christ was faithful as a son placed
> over his house. We are his house,
> if only we hold fast to our confidence
> and pride in our hope.
> Hebrews 3:6

Day 144

Before Father God I decree, and I declare in the name of Jesus Christ of Nazareth, that you, *my baby*, will hear Jesus's voice today and forever.

Thank You, Father. I praise You, Father. I worship You, Father. Thank You, Jesus. I praise You, Jesus. I worship You, Jesus. Thank You, Holy Spirit. I praise You, Holy Spirit. I worship You, Holy Spirit.
Amen.

> Therefore, as the holy Spirit says:
> Oh, that today you would hear his voice.
> Hebrews 3:7

Day 145

Before Father God I decree, and I declare in the name of Jesus Christ of Nazareth, that you, *my baby*, will encourage yourself and others in Christ.

Thank You, Father. I praise You, Father. I worship You, Father.
Thank You, Jesus. I praise You, Jesus. I worship You, Jesus.
Thank You, Holy Spirit. I praise You, Holy Spirit. I worship You, Holy Spirit.
Amen.

Encourage yourselves daily while it is still "today,"
so that none of you may grow
hardened by the deceit of sin.
Hebrews 3:13

Day 146

Before Father God I decree, and I declare in the name of Jesus Christ of Nazareth, that you, *my baby*, have become a partner of Christ. You will hold the beginning of the reality firm until the end.

Thank You, Father. I praise You, Father. I worship You, Father.
Thank You, Jesus. I praise You, Jesus. I worship You, Jesus.
Thank You, Holy Spirit. I praise You, Holy Spirit. I worship You, Holy Spirit.
Amen.

We have become partners of Christ if only we hold
the beginning of the reality firm until the end.
Hebrews 3:14

Day 147

Before Father God I decree, and I declare in the name of Jesus Christ of Nazareth, that you, *my baby*, have received the good news and benefited from it.

Thank You, Father. I praise You, Father. I worship You, Father. Thank You, Jesus. I praise You, Jesus. I worship You, Jesus. Thank You, Holy Spirit. I praise You, Holy Spirit. I worship You, Holy Spirit.
Amen.

For in fact we have received the good news just as they did.
But the word that they heard did not profit them,
for they were not united in faith with those who listened.
Hebrews 4:2

Day 148

Before Father God I decree, and I declare in the name of Jesus Christ of Nazareth, that you, *my baby*, will enter into God's rest, resting from your own works as God did from His.

Thank You, Father. I praise You, Father. I worship You, Father. Thank You, Jesus. I praise You, Jesus. I worship You, Jesus. Thank You, Holy Spirit. I praise You, Holy Spirit. I worship You, Holy Spirit.
Amen.

And whoever enters into God's rest, rests from
his own works as God did from his.
Hebrews 4:10

Day 149

Before Father God I decree, and I declare in the name of Jesus Christ of Nazareth, that you, *my baby*, have received the Word of God. The Word of God is living and effective, sharper than any two-edged sword, penetrating even between soul and spirit.

Thank You, Father. I praise You, Father. I worship You, Father. Thank You, Jesus. I praise You, Jesus. I worship You, Jesus. Thank You, Holy Spirit. I praise You, Holy Spirit. I worship You, Holy Spirit.
Amen.

> Indeed, the word of God is living and effective,
> sharper than any two-edged sword,
> penetrating even between soul and
> spirit, joints and marrow,
> and able to discern reflections and thoughts of the heart.
> Hebrews 4:12

Day 150

Before Father God I decree, and I declare in the name of Jesus Christ of Nazareth, that you, *my baby*, have the right to come boldly before the throne of God to find mercy and grace in a time of need.

Thank You, Father. I praise You, Father. I worship You, Father. Thank You, Jesus. I praise You, Jesus. I worship You, Jesus. Thank You, Holy Spirit. I praise You, Holy Spirit. I worship You, Holy Spirit.
Amen.

> So let us confidently approach the throne of grace
> to receive mercy and to find grace for timely help.
> Hebrews 4:16

Day 151

Before Father God I decree, and I declare in the name of Jesus Christ of Nazareth, that you, *my baby*, have faculties trained by practice to discern good and evil.

Thank You, Father. I praise You, Father. I worship You, Father. Thank You, Jesus. I praise You, Jesus. I worship You, Jesus. Thank You, Holy Spirit. I praise You, Holy Spirit. I worship You, Holy Spirit.
Amen.

But solid food is for the mature, for those whose faculties are trained by practice to discern good and evil.
Hebrews 5:14

Day 152

Before Father God I decree, and I declare in the name of Jesus Christ of Nazareth, that you, *my baby*, will enter with confidence through the blood of Jesus into the sanctuary.

Thank You, Father. I praise You, Father. I worship You, Father. Thank You, Jesus. I praise You, Jesus. I worship You, Jesus. Thank You, Holy Spirit. I praise You, Holy Spirit. I worship You, Holy Spirit.
Amen.

Therefore, brothers, … through the blood of Jesus we have confidence of entrance into the sanctuary.
Hebrews 10:19

Day 153

Before Father God I decree, and I declare in the name of Jesus Christ of Nazareth, that you, *my baby*, have received the new and living way which Jesus opened for you through the veil, that is, Jesus's body.

Thank You, Father. I praise You, Father. I worship You, Father. Thank You, Jesus. I praise You, Jesus. I worship You, Jesus. Thank You, Holy Spirit. I praise You, Holy Spirit. I worship You, Holy Spirit.
Amen.

By the new and living way he opened for
us through the veil, that is, his flesh.
Hebrews 10:20

Day 154

Before Father God I decree, and I declare in the name of Jesus Christ of Nazareth, that you, *my baby*, will approach Jesus with a sincere heart, sprinkled clean from an evil conscience and your body washed in pure water.

Thank You, Father. I praise You, Father. I worship You, Father. Thank You, Jesus. I praise You, Jesus. I worship You, Jesus. Thank You, Holy Spirit. I praise You, Holy Spirit. I worship You, Holy Spirit.
Amen.

Let us approach with a sincere heart and in absolute trust,
with our hearts sprinkled clean from an evil conscience
and our bodies washed in pure water.
Hebrews 10:22

Day 155

Before Father God I decree, and I declare in the name of Jesus Christ of Nazareth, that you, *my baby*, are a hearer and doer of the word.

Thank You, Father. I praise You, Father. I worship You, Father. Thank You, Jesus. I praise You, Jesus. I worship You, Jesus. Thank You, Holy Spirit. I praise You, Holy Spirit. I worship You, Holy Spirit.
Amen.

> For if anyone is a hearer of the word and not a doer,
> he is like a man who looks at his own face in a mirror.
> James 1:23

Day 156

Before Father God I decree, and I declare in the name of Jesus Christ of Nazareth, that you, *my baby*, will submit yourself to God. You will resist the devil, and he will flee from you.

Thank You God, I praise You God, I worship You God. Thank You, Father. I praise You, Father. I worship You, Father. Thank You, Jesus. I praise You, Jesus. I worship You, Jesus. Thank You, Holy Spirit. I praise You, Holy Spirit. I worship You, Holy Spirit.
Amen.

> So submit yourselves to God. Resist the
> devil, and he will flee from you.
> James 4:7

Day 157

Before Father God I decree, and I declare in the name of Jesus Christ of Nazareth, that you, *my baby*, will draw near to God and God will draw near to you.

Thank You, Father. I praise You, Father. I worship You, Father. Thank You, Jesus. I praise You, Jesus. I worship You, Jesus. Thank You, Holy Spirit. I praise You, Holy Spirit. I worship You, Holy Spirit.
Amen.

Draw near to God, and he will draw near to you.
James 4:8

Day 158

Before Father God I decree, and I declare in the name of Jesus Christ of Nazareth, that you, *my baby*, will humble yourself before the Lord and He will exalt you.

Thank You, Father. I praise You, Father. I worship You, Father. Thank You, Jesus. I praise You, Jesus. I worship You, Jesus. Thank You, Holy Spirit. I praise You, Holy Spirit. I worship You, Holy Spirit.
Amen.

Humble yourselves before the Lord and he will exalt you.
James 4:10

Day 159

Before Father God I decree, and I declare in the name of Jesus Christ of Nazareth, that you, *my baby*, have been born anew from imperishable seed through the living and abiding Word of God.

Thank You, Father. I praise You, Father. I worship You, Father. Thank You, Jesus. I praise You, Jesus. I worship You, Jesus. Thank You, Holy Spirit. I praise You, Holy Spirit. I worship You, Holy Spirit.
Amen.

> You have been born anew, not from
> perishable but from imperishable seed,
> through the living and abiding word of God.
> 1 Peter 1:23

Day 160

Before Father God I decree, and I declare in the name of Jesus Christ of Nazareth, that you, *my baby*, have tasted that the Lord is good.

Thank You, Father. I praise You, Father. I worship You, Father. Thank You, Jesus. I praise You, Jesus. I worship You, Jesus. Thank You, Holy Spirit. I praise You, Holy Spirit. I worship You, Holy Spirit.
Amen.

> For you have tasted that the Lord is good.
> 1 Peter 2:3

Day 161

Before Father God I decree, and I declare in the name of Jesus Christ of Nazareth, that you, my baby, are one of God's living stones, being built up in Christ as a spiritual house.

Thank You, Father. I praise You, Father. I worship You, Father. Thank You, Jesus. I praise You, Jesus. I worship You, Jesus. Thank You, Holy Spirit. I praise You, Holy Spirit. I worship You, Holy Spirit.
Amen.

> And like living stones, let yourselves
> be built into a spiritual house
> to be a holy priesthood to offer spiritual sacrifices
> acceptable to God through Jesus Christ.
> 1 Peter 2:5

Day 162

Before Father God I decree, and I declare in the name of Jesus Christ of Nazareth, that you, *my baby*, are a member of a chosen race, a royal priesthood, a holy nation, a people for God's own possession.

Thank You, Father. I praise You, Father. I worship You, Father. Thank You, Jesus. I praise You, Jesus. I worship You, Jesus. Thank You, Holy Spirit. I praise You, Holy Spirit. I worship You, Holy Spirit.
Amen.

> But you are "a chosen race, a royal
> priesthood, a holy nation,
> a people of his own, so that you may announce the praises"
> of him who called you out of darkness
> into his wonderful light.
> 1 Peter 2:9

Day 163

Before Father God I decree, and I declare in the name of Jesus Christ of Nazareth, that you, *my baby*, will humble yourself under the mighty hand of God, and He will exalt you in due time.

Thank You, Father. I praise You, Father. I worship You, Father. Thank You, Jesus. I praise You, Jesus. I worship You, Jesus. Thank You, Holy Spirit. I praise You, Holy Spirit. I worship You, Holy Spirit.
Amen.

So humble yourselves under the mighty hand of God,
that he may exalt you in due time.
1 Peter 5:6

Day 164

Before Father God I decree, and I declare in the name of Jesus Christ of Nazareth, that you, *my baby*, will cast all your worries upon God, because He cares for you.

Thank You, Father. I praise You, Father. I worship You, Father. Thank You, Jesus. I praise You, Jesus. I worship You, Jesus. Thank You, Holy Spirit. I praise You, Holy Spirit. I worship You, Holy Spirit.
Amen.

Cast all your worries upon him because he cares for you.
1 Peter 5:7

Day 165

Before Father God I decree, and I declare in the name of Jesus Christ of Nazareth, that you, *my baby*, have been called by the God of all grace to His eternal glory through Christ Jesus.

Thank You, Father. I praise You, Father. I worship You, Father.
Thank You, Jesus. I praise You, Jesus. I worship You, Jesus.
Thank You, Holy Spirit. I praise You, Holy Spirit. I worship You, Holy Spirit.
Amen.

The God of all grace who called you to his
eternal glory through Christ Jesus
will himself restore, confirm, strengthen, and establish you
after you have suffered a little.
1 Peter 5:10

Day 166

Before Father God I decree, and I declare in the name of Jesus Christ of Nazareth, that you, *my baby*, partake of God's divine nature.

Thank You, Father. I praise You, Father. I worship You, Father.
Thank You, Jesus. I praise You, Jesus. I worship You, Jesus.
Thank You, Holy Spirit. I praise You, Holy Spirit. I worship You, Holy Spirit.
Amen.

Through these, he has bestowed on us the
precious and very great promises,
so that through them you may come
to share in the divine nature,
after escaping from the corruption that is
in the world because of evil desire.
2 Peter 1:4

Day 167

Before Father God I decree, and I declare in the name of Jesus Christ of Nazareth, that you, *my baby*, have been given exceedingly great and precious promises.

Thank You, Father. I praise You, Father. I worship You, Father. Thank You, Jesus. I praise You, Jesus. I worship You, Jesus. Thank You, Holy Spirit. I praise You, Holy Spirit. I worship You, Holy Spirit.
Amen.

> Through these, he has bestowed on us the
> precious and very great promises,
> so that through them you may come
> to share in the divine nature,
> after escaping from the corruption that is
> in the world because of evil desire.
> 2 Peter 1:4

Day 168

Before Father God I decree, and I declare in the name of Jesus Christ of Nazareth, that you, *my baby*, have been richly provided for by the Lord and Savior Jesus Christ. You will enter into the eternal kingdom.

Thank You, Father. I praise You, Father. I worship You, Father. Thank You, Jesus. I praise You, Jesus. I worship You, Jesus. Thank You, Holy Spirit. I praise You, Holy Spirit. I worship You, Holy Spirit.
Amen.

> For, in this way, entry into eternal kingdom
> of our Lord and savior Jesus Christ
> will be richly provided for you.
> 2 Peter 1:11

Day 169

Before Father God I decree, and I declare in the name of Jesus Christ of Nazareth, that you, *my baby*, have heard from Jesus and you will proclaim God is light and in Him there is no darkness at all.

Thank You, Father. I praise You, Father. I worship You, Father. Thank You, Jesus. I praise You, Jesus. I worship You, Jesus. Thank You, Holy Spirit. I praise You, Holy Spirit. I worship You, Holy Spirit.
Amen.

> Now this is the message that we have heard from him
> and proclaim to you: God is light, and in
> him there is no darkness at all.
> 1 John 1:5

Day 170

Before Father God I decree, and I declare in the name of Jesus Christ of Nazareth, that you, *my baby*, are walking in the light and God is in the light. You have fellowship with God, and the blood of His Son Jesus cleanses you from all sin.

Thank You, Father. I praise You, Father. I worship You, Father. Thank You, Jesus. I praise You, Jesus. I worship You, Jesus. Thank You, Holy Spirit. I praise You, Holy Spirit. I worship You, Holy Spirit.
Amen.

> But if we walk in the light as he is in the light,
> then we have fellowship with one another,
> and the blood of his Son Jesus cleanses us from all sin.
> 1 John 1:7

Day 171

Before Father God I decree, and I declare in the name of Jesus Christ of Nazareth, that you, *my baby*, have kept the Word of God, and God's love is truly perfected in you. You are in union with God.

Thank You, Father. I praise You, Father. I worship You, Father. Thank You, Jesus. I praise You, Jesus. I worship You, Jesus. Thank You, Holy Spirit. I praise You, Holy Spirit. I worship You, Holy Spirit.
Amen.

> But whoever keeps his word, the love of
> God is truly perfected in him.
> This is the way we may know that
> we are in union with him.
> 1 John 2:5

Day 172

Before Father God I decree, and I declare in the name of Jesus Christ of Nazareth, that you, *my baby*, abide in Jesus and ought to live as He lived.

Thank You, Father. I praise You, Father. I worship You, Father. Thank You, Jesus. I praise You, Jesus. I worship You, Jesus. Thank You, Holy Spirit. I praise You, Holy Spirit. I worship You, Holy Spirit.
Amen.

> Whoever claims to abide in him
> ought to live just as he lived.
> 1 John 2:6

Day 173

Before Father God I decree, and I declare in the name of Jesus Christ of Nazareth, that you, *my baby*, are a child of God and your sins are forgiven for Jesus's name's sake.

Thank You, Father. I praise You, Father. I worship You, Father. Thank You, Jesus. I praise You, Jesus. I worship You, Jesus. Thank You, Holy Spirit. I praise You, Holy Spirit. I worship You, Holy Spirit.
Amen.

> I am writing to you, children, because your sins
> have been forgiven for his name's sake.
> 1 John 2:12

Day 174

Before Father God I decree, and I declare in the name of Jesus Christ of Nazareth, that you, *my baby*, know God, who is from the beginning, and you have conquered the evil one.

Thank You, Father. I praise You, Father. I worship You, Father. Thank You, Jesus. I praise You, Jesus. I worship You, Jesus. Thank You, Holy Spirit. I praise You, Holy Spirit. I worship You, Holy Spirit.
Amen.

> I am writing to you, fathers, because you
> know him who is from the beginning.
> I am writing to you, young men, because
> you have conquered the evil one.
> 1 John 2:13

Day 175

Before Father God I decree, and I declare in the name of Jesus Christ of Nazareth, that you, *my baby*, know the Father. You are strong, and the Word of God remains in you, and you have conquered the evil one.

Thank You, Father. I praise You, Father. I worship You, Father. Thank You, Jesus. I praise You, Jesus. I worship You, Jesus. Thank You, Holy Spirit. I praise You, Holy Spirit. I worship You, Holy Spirit.
Amen.

I write to you, children, because you know the Father …
I write to you, young men, because you are
strong and the word of God remains in you,
and you have conquered the evil one.
1 John 2:14

Day 176

Before Father God I decree, and I declare in the name of Jesus Christ of Nazareth, that you, *my baby*, will do the will of God and remain forever.

Thank You, Father. I praise You, Father. I worship You, Father. Thank You, Jesus. I praise You, Jesus. I worship You, Jesus. Thank You, Holy Spirit. I praise You, Holy Spirit. I worship You, Holy Spirit.
Amen.

Yet the world and its enticement are passing away.
But whoever does the will of God remains forever.
1 John 2:17

Day 177

Before Father God I decree, and I declare in the name of Jesus Christ of Nazareth, that you, *my baby*, have the anointing that comes from the holy one, and you have knowledge.

Thank You, Father. I praise You, Father. I worship You, Father. Thank You, Jesus. I praise You, Jesus. I worship You, Jesus. Thank You, Holy Spirit. I praise You, Holy Spirit. I worship You, Holy Spirit.
Amen.

> But you have the anointing that comes from
> the holy one, and you all have knowledge.
> 1 John 2:20

Day 178

Before Father God I decree, and I declare in the name of Jesus Christ of Nazareth, that you, *my baby*, will always confess the Son and have the Father as well.

Thank You, Father. I praise You, Father. I worship You, Father. Thank You, Jesus. I praise You, Jesus. I worship You, Jesus. Thank You, Holy Spirit. I praise You, Holy Spirit. I worship You, Holy Spirit.
Amen.

> No one who denies the Son has the Father, but
> whoever confesses the Son has the Father as well.
> 1 John 2:23

Day 179

Before Father God I decree, and I declare in the name of Jesus Christ of Nazareth, that you, *my baby*, will remain in the Son and in the Father, and that what you heard from the beginning will remain in you.

Thank You, Father. I praise You, Father. I worship You, Father. Thank You, Jesus. I praise You, Jesus. I worship You, Jesus. Thank You, Holy Spirit. I praise You, Holy Spirit. I worship You, Holy Spirit.
Amen.

Let what you heard from the beginning remain in you.
If what you heard from the beginning remains in you,
then you will remain in the Son and in the Father.
1 John 2:24

Day 180

Before Father God I decree, and I declare in the name of Jesus Christ of Nazareth, that you, *my baby*, are anointed by God and anointing will teach you.

Thank You, Father. I praise You, Father. I worship You, Father. Thank You, Jesus. I praise You, Jesus. I worship You, Jesus. Thank You, Holy Spirit. I praise You, Holy Spirit. I worship You, Holy Spirit.
Amen.

As for you, the anointing that you received
from him remains in you,
so that you do not need anyone to teach you.
But his anointing teaches you about
everything and is true and not false;
just as it taught you, remain in him.
1 John 2:27

Day 181

Before Father God I decree, and I declare in the name of Jesus Christ of Nazareth, that you, *my baby*, have hope based on God and you are pure like God.

Thank You, Father. I praise You, Father. I worship You, Father. Thank You, Jesus. I praise You, Jesus. I worship You, Jesus. Thank You, Holy Spirit. I praise You, Holy Spirit. I worship You, Holy Spirit.
Amen.

> Everyone who has this hope based on him
> makes himself pure, as he is pure.
> 1 John 3:3

Day 182

Before Father God I decree, and I declare in the name of Jesus Christ of Nazareth, that you, *my baby*, will love others.

Thank You, Father. I praise You, Father. I worship You, Father. Thank You, Jesus. I praise You, Jesus. I worship You, Jesus. Thank You, Holy Spirit. I praise You, Holy Spirit. I worship You, Holy Spirit.
Amen.

> For this is the message you have heard from the beginning;
> we should love one another.
> 1 John 3:11

Day 183

Before Father God I decree, and I declare in the name of Jesus Christ of Nazareth, that you, *my baby*, will receive from God whatever you ask because you keep his commandments and do what pleases God.

Thank You, Father. I praise You, Father. I worship You, Father. Thank You, Jesus. I praise You, Jesus. I worship You, Jesus. Thank You, Holy Spirit. I praise You, Holy Spirit. I worship You, Holy Spirit.
Amen.

> And receive from him whatever we ask,
> because we keep his commandments
> and do what please him.
> 1 John 3:22

Day 184

Before Father God I decree, and I declare in the name of Jesus Christ of Nazareth, that you, *my baby*, are loved by God.

Thank You, Father. I praise You, Father. I worship You, Father. Thank You, Jesus. I praise You, Jesus. I worship You, Jesus. Thank You, Holy Spirit. I praise You, Holy Spirit. I worship You, Holy Spirit.
Amen.

> In this is love: not that we have loved
> God, but that he loved us
> and sent his Son as expiation for our sins.
> 1 John 4:10

Day 185

Before Father God I decree, and I declare in the name of Jesus Christ of Nazareth, that you, *my baby*, are like Christ.

Thank You, Father. I praise You, Father. I worship You, Father. Thank You, Jesus. I praise You, Jesus. I worship You, Jesus. Thank You, Holy Spirit. I praise You, Holy Spirit. I worship You, Holy Spirit.
Amen.

Beloved, we are God's children now; what
we shall be has not yet been revealed.
We do know that when it is revealed we shall
be like him, for we shall see him as he is.
1 John 3.2

Day 186

Before Father God I decree, and I declare in the name of Jesus Christ of Nazareth, that you, *my baby*, have life because you possess the Son.

Thank You, Father. I praise You, Father. I worship You, Father. Thank You, Jesus. I praise You, Jesus. I worship You, Jesus. Thank You, Holy Spirit. I praise You, Holy Spirit. I worship You, Holy Spirit.
Amen.

Whoever possesses the Son has life,
whoever does not possess the Son
of God does not have life.
1 John 5:12

Day 187

Before Father God I decree, and I declare in the name of Jesus Christ of Nazareth, that you, *my baby*, are a recipient of all God's promises.

Thank You, Father. I praise You, Father. I worship You, Father. Thank You, Jesus. I praise You, Jesus. I worship You, Jesus. Thank You, Holy Spirit. I praise You, Holy Spirit. I worship You, Holy Spirit.
Amen.

> Through these, he has bestowed on us the
> precious and very great promises,
> so that through them you may come
> to share in the divine nature,
> after escaping from the corruption that is
> in the world because of evil desire.
> 2 Peter 1:4

Day 188

Before Father God I decree, and I declare in the name of Jesus Christ of Nazareth, that you, *my baby*, are anointed king over Israel.

Thank You, Father. I praise You, Father. I worship You, Father. Thank You, Jesus. I praise You, Jesus. I worship You, Jesus. Thank You, Holy Spirit. I praise You, Holy Spirit. I worship You, Holy Spirit.
Amen.

> From the flask you have, pour oil on his head, and say,
> "Thus says the LORD: I anoint you king over Israel."
> Then open the door and flee without delay.
> 2 Kings 9:3

Day 189

Before Father God I decree, and I declare in the name of Jesus Christ of Nazareth, that you, *my baby*, are the anointed ruler over God's inheritance.

Thank You, Father. I praise You, Father. I worship You, Father. Thank You, Jesus. I praise You, Jesus. I worship You, Jesus. Thank You, Holy Spirit. I praise You, Holy Spirit. I worship You, Holy Spirit.
Amen.

Then, from a flask he had with him,
Samuel poured oil on Saul's head
and kissed him, saying: "The LORD anoints
you ruler over his people Israel.
You are the one who will govern the
LORD's people and save them
from the power of their enemies all around them."
1 Samuel 10:1

Day 190

Before Father God I decree, and I declare in the name of Jesus Christ of Nazareth, that you, *my baby,* are pointed out by God.

Thank You, Father. I praise You, Father. I worship You, Father. Thank You, Jesus. I praise You, Jesus. I worship You, Jesus. Thank You, Holy Spirit. I praise You, Holy Spirit. I worship You, Holy Spirit.
Amen.

Invite Jesse to the sacrifice, and I
myself will tell you what to do;
you are to anoint for me the one I point out to you.
1 Samuel 16:3b

Day 191

Before Father God I decree, and I declare in the name of Jesus Christ of Nazareth, that you, *my baby*, have been anointed by God. The Spirit of the Lord is upon you.

Thank You, Father. I praise You, Father. I worship You, Father. Thank You, Jesus. I praise You, Jesus. I worship You, Jesus. Thank You, Holy Spirit. I praise You, Holy Spirit. I worship You, Holy Spirit.
Amen.

> The spirit of the Lord God is upon me,
> because the Lord has anointed me.
> Isaiah 61:1

Day 192

Before Father God I decree, and I declare in the name of Jesus Christ of Nazareth, that you, *my baby*, have been sent to bring good news to the afflicted, to bind up the brokenhearted, to proclaim liberty to the captives, release to the prisoners.

Thank You, Father. I praise You, Father. I worship You, Father. Thank You, Jesus. I praise You, Jesus. I worship You, Jesus. Thank You, Holy Spirit. I praise You, Holy Spirit. I worship You, Holy Spirit.
Amen.

> He has sent me to bring good news to the afflicted,
> to bind up the brokenhearted.
> To proclaim liberty to the captives,
> release to the prisoners.
> Isaiah 61:1

Day 193

Before Father God I decree, and I declare in the name of Jesus Christ of Nazareth, that you, *my baby*, will announce a year of favor from the Lord and a day of vindication by God. You will comfort all who mourn.

Thank You, Father. I praise You, Father. I worship You, Father. Thank You, Jesus. I praise You, Jesus. I worship You, Jesus. Thank You, Holy Spirit. I praise You, Holy Spirit. I worship You, Holy Spirit.
Amen.

> He has sent me ...
> To announce a year of favor from the LORD
> and a day of vindication by our God;
> To comfort all who mourn.
> Isaiah 61:1–2

Day 194

Before Father God I decree, and I declare in the name of Jesus Christ of Nazareth, that you, *my baby*, are clothed in glorious mantle and anointed with oil of gladness.

Thank You, Father. I praise You, Father. I worship You, Father. Thank You, Jesus. I praise You, Jesus. I worship You, Jesus. Thank You, Holy Spirit. I praise You, Holy Spirit. I worship You, Holy Spirit.
Amen.

> To place on those who mourn in Zion
> a diadem instead of ashes.
> To give them oil of gladness instead of mourning,
> a glorious mantle instead of a faint spirit.
> Isaiah 61:3a

Day 195

Before Father God I decree, and I declare in the name of Jesus Christ of Nazareth, that you, *my baby*, will be called an oak of justice. You are planted by the Lord to show His glory.

Thank You, Father. I praise You, Father. I worship You, Father. Thank You, Jesus. I praise You, Jesus. I worship You, Jesus. Thank You, Holy Spirit. I praise You, Holy Spirit. I worship You, Holy Spirit.
Amen.

They will be called oaks of justice,
the planting of the LORD to show his glory.
Isaiah 61:3b

Day 196

Before Father God I decree, and I declare in the name of Jesus Christ of Nazareth, that you, my baby, will rebuild the ancient ruins and restore desolate cities.

Thank You, Father. I praise You, Father. I worship You, Father. Thank You, Jesus. I praise You, Jesus. I worship You, Jesus. Thank You, Holy Spirit. I praise You, Holy Spirit. I worship You, Holy Spirit.
Amen.

Isaiah 61:4
They shall rebuild the ancient ruins,
the former wastes they shall raise up
And restore the desolate cities,
devastation of generation upon generation.

Day 197

Before Father God I decree, and I declare in the name of Jesus Christ of Nazareth, that you, *my baby*, are a priest of the Lord and a minister of our God.

Thank You, Father. I praise You, Father. I worship You, Father. Thank You, Jesus. I praise You, Jesus. I worship You, Jesus. Thank You, Holy Spirit. I praise You, Holy Spirit. I worship You, Holy Spirit.
Amen.

> You yourself shall be called "Priests of the LORD,"
> "Ministers of our God" you shall be called.
> Isaiah 61:6a

Day 198

Before Father God I decree, and I declare in the name of Jesus Christ of Nazareth, that you, *my baby*, will eat the wealth of the nations and boast in their riches.

Thank You, Father. I praise You, Father. I worship You, Father. Thank You, Jesus. I praise You, Jesus. I worship You, Jesus. Thank You, Holy Spirit. I praise You, Holy Spirit. I worship You, Holy Spirit.
Amen.

> You shall eat the wealth of the nations
> and in their riches you will boast. Isaiah 61:6b

Day 199

Before Father God I decree, and I declare in the name of Jesus Christ of Nazareth, that you, *my baby*, and your generation will always receive faithful recompense. God will make covenant with you and your generation.

Thank You, Father. I praise You, Father. I worship You, Father. Thank You, Jesus. I praise You, Jesus. I worship You, Jesus. Thank You, Holy Spirit. I praise You, Holy Spirit. I worship You, Holy Spirit.
Amen.

For, I, the LORD, love justice,
I hate robbery and wrongdoing;
I will faithfully give them their recompense,
an everlasting covenant I will make with them.
Isaiah 61: 8

Day 200

Before Father God I decree, and I declare in the name of Jesus Christ of Nazareth, that you, *my baby*, and your offspring shall be renowned among the nations. All who see you will acknowledge you and them; they will call you blessed.

Thank You, Father. I praise You, Father. I worship You, Father. Thank You, Jesus. I praise You, Jesus. I worship You, Jesus. Thank You, Holy Spirit. I praise You, Holy Spirit. I worship You, Holy Spirit.
Amen.

Their offspring shall be renowned among the nations.
and their descendants in the midst of the peoples;
All who see them shall acknowledge them:
"They are offspring the LORD has blessed."
Isaiah 61:9

Day 201

Before Father God I decree, and I declare in the name of Jesus Christ of Nazareth, that you, *my baby*, will rejoice heartily in the Lord.

Thank You, Father. I praise You, Father. I worship You, Father. Thank You, Jesus. I praise You, Jesus. I worship You, Jesus. Thank You, Holy Spirit. I praise You, Holy Spirit. I worship You, Holy Spirit.
Amen.

I will greatly rejoice in the Lord,
my whole being shall exult in my God.
Isaiah 61:10 (NRSV)

Day 202

Before Father God I decree, and I declare in the name of Jesus Christ of Nazareth, that you, *my baby*, are clothed with garment of salvations. You are wrapped in a robe of justice.

Thank You, Father. I praise You, Father. I worship You, Father. Thank You, Jesus. I praise You, Jesus. I worship You, Jesus. Thank You, Holy Spirit. I praise You, Holy Spirit. I worship You, Holy Spirit.
Amen.

For he has clothed me with the garments of salvation,
he has covered me with the robe of righteousness,
as a bridegroom decks himself with a garland,
and as a bride adorns herself with her jewels.
Isaiah 61:10 (NRSV)

Day 203

Before Father God I decree, and I declare in the name of Jesus Christ of Nazareth, that you, *my baby*, are a glorious crown in the hand of the Lord, a royal diadem in the hand of your God.

Thank You, Father. I praise You, Father. I worship You, Father. Thank You, Jesus. I praise You, Jesus. I worship You, Jesus. Thank You, Holy Spirit. I praise You, Holy Spirit. I worship You, Holy Spirit.
Amen.

You shall be a crown of beauty in the hand of the Lord,
and a royal diadem in the hand of your God.
Isaiah 62:3 (NRSV)

Day 204

Before Father God I decree, and I declare in the name of Jesus Christ of Nazareth, that you, *my baby*, are clay; you are the work of God's hand. God is your Father and Potter.

Thank You, Father. I praise You, Father. I worship You, Father. Thank You, Jesus. I praise You, Jesus. I worship You, Jesus. Thank You, Holy Spirit. I praise You, Holy Spirit. I worship You, Holy Spirit.
Amen.

Yet, O Lord, you are our father;
we are the clay and you our potter;
we are all the work of your hand.
Isaiah 64:7 (NRVS)

Day 205

Before Father God I decree, and I declare in the name of Jesus Christ of Nazareth, that you, *my baby*, have an anointed mouth. God placed His words in your mouth.

Thank You, Father. I praise You, Father. I worship You, Father. Thank You, Jesus. I praise You, Jesus. I worship You, Jesus. Thank You, Holy Spirit. I praise You, Holy Spirit. I worship You, Holy Spirit.
Amen.

> Than the LORD put out his hand and touched my mouth;
> and the LORD said to me, "Now I have
> put my words in your mouth."
> Jeremiah 1:9 (NRSV)

Day 206

Before Father God I decree, and I declare in the name of Jesus Christ of Nazareth, that you, *my baby*, are appointed over nations and over kingdoms to build and to plant.

Thank You, Father. I praise You, Father. I worship You, Father. Thank You, Jesus. I praise You, Jesus. I worship You, Jesus. Thank You, Holy Spirit. I praise You, Holy Spirit. I worship You, Holy Spirit.
Amen.

> See, today I appoint you over nations and over kingdoms,
> to pluck up and to pull down, to destroy and to overthrow,
> to build and to plant.
> Jeremiah 1:10 (NRSV)

Day 207

Before Father God I decree, and I declare in the name of Jesus Christ of Nazareth, that you, *my baby*, are a fortified city, a pillar of iron, and a wall of bronze.

Thank You, Father. I praise You, Father. I worship You, Father. Thank You, Jesus. I praise You, Jesus. I worship You, Jesus. Thank You, Holy Spirit. I praise You, Holy Spirit. I worship You, Holy Spirit.
Amen.

And I for my part have made you today a fortified city,
an iron pillar, and a bronze wall, against the whole land—
against the kings of Judah, its princes, its
priests, and the people of the land.
Jeremiah 1:18 (NRSV)

Day 208

Before Father God I decree, and I declare in the name of Jesus Christ of Nazareth, that you, *my baby*, have received a heart from God to know Him.

Thank You, Father. I praise You, Father. I worship You, Father. Thank You, Jesus. I praise You, Jesus. I worship You, Jesus. Thank You, Holy Spirit. I praise You, Holy Spirit. I worship You, Holy Spirit.
Amen.

I will give them a heart to know that I am the LORD:
and they shall be my people and I will be their God,
for they shall return to me with their whole heart.
Jeremiah 24:7 (NRSV)

Day 209

Before Father God I decree, and I declare in the name of Jesus Christ of Nazareth, that you, *my baby*, are anointed with the Holy Spirit and power. You will do good and heal those oppressed by the devil. God is with you.

Thank You, Father. I praise You, Father. I worship You, Father. Thank You, Jesus. I praise You, Jesus. I worship You, Jesus. Thank You, Holy Spirit. I praise You, Holy Spirit. I worship You, Holy Spirit.
Amen.

God anointed Jesus of Nazareth with
the holy Spirit and with power;
how he went about doing good and healing all
who were oppressed by the devil, for God was with him.
Acts 10:38 (NRSV)

Day 210

Before Father God I decree, and I declare in the name of Jesus Christ of Nazareth, that you, *my baby*, have courage through God, the gospel in spite of opposition.

Thank You, Father. I praise You, Father. I worship You, Father. Thank You, Jesus. I praise You, Jesus. I worship You, Jesus. Thank You, Holy Spirit. I praise You, Holy Spirit. I worship You, Holy Spirit.
Amen.

But though we had already suffered and
been shamefully mistreated
at Philippi, as you know, we had courage
in our God to declare to you
the gospel of God in spite of great opposition.
1 Thessalonians 2:2 (NRSV)

Day 211

Before Father God I decree, and I declare in the name of Jesus Christ of Nazareth, that you, *my baby*, are strengthened and encouraged in faith by gospel of Christ.

Thank You, Father. I praise You, Father. I worship You, Father. Thank You, Jesus. I praise You, Jesus. I worship You, Jesus. Thank You, Holy Spirit. I praise You, Holy Spirit. I worship You, Holy Spirit.
Amen.

And we sent Timothy, our brother and co-worker for God
in proclaiming the gospel of Christ, to
strengthen and encourage
you for the sake of your faith.
1 Thessalonians 3:2 (NRSV)

Day 212

Before Father God I decree, and I declare in the name of Jesus Christ of Nazareth, that you, *my baby*, receive every desire of your heart and have all your plans fulfilled.

Thank You, Father. I praise You, Father. I worship You, Father. Thank You, Jesus. I praise You, Jesus. I worship You, Jesus. Thank You, Holy Spirit. I praise You, Holy Spirit. I worship You, Holy Spirit.
Amen.

May he grant you your heart's desire,
and fulfill all your plans.
Psalm 20:4 (NRSV)

Day 213

Before Father God I decree, and I declare in the name of Jesus Christ of Nazareth, that you, *my baby*, are granted every petition.

Thank You, Father. I praise You, Father. I worship You, Father. Thank You, Jesus. I praise You, Jesus. I worship You, Jesus. Thank You, Holy Spirit. I praise You, Holy Spirit. I worship You, Holy Spirit.
Amen.

May we shout for joy over your victory,
and in the name of our God set up our banners.
May the LORD fulfill all your petitions.
Psalm 20:5 (NRSV)

Day 214

Before Father God I decree, and I declare in the name of Jesus Christ of Nazareth, that you, *my baby*, will receive help from God because you are His anointed.

Thank You, Father. I praise You, Father. I worship You, Father. Thank You, Jesus. I praise You, Jesus. I worship You, Jesus. Thank You, Holy Spirit. I praise You, Holy Spirit. I worship You, Holy Spirit.
Amen.

Now I know that the LORD will help his anointed.
Psalm 20:6 (NRSV)

Day 215

Before Father God I decree, and I declare in the name of Jesus Christ of Nazareth, that you, *my baby,* will be protected by God from enemies and persecutors.

Thank You, Father. I praise You, Father. I worship You, Father. Thank You, Jesus. I praise You, Jesus. I worship You, Jesus. Thank You, Holy Spirit. I praise You, Holy Spirit. I worship You, Holy Spirit.
Amen.

> My times are in your hand; deliver me from
> the hand of my enemies and persecutors.
> Psalm 31:15 (NRSV)

Day 216

Before Father God I decree, and I declare in the name of Jesus Christ of Nazareth, that you, *my baby*, have refuge in God's wings.

Thank You, Father. I praise You, Father. I worship You, Father. Thank You, Jesus. I praise You, Jesus. I worship You, Jesus. Thank You, Holy Spirit. I praise You, Holy Spirit. I worship You, Holy Spirit.
Amen.

> How precious is your steadfast love, O God!
> All people may take refuge in the shadow of your wings.
> Psalm 36:7 (NRSV)

Day 217

Before Father God I decree, and I declare in the name of Jesus Christ of Nazareth, that you, *my baby*, will serve the Lord and He will bless your food and drink. He will remove sickness from your family.

Thank You, Father. I praise You, Father. I worship You, Father. Thank You, Jesus. I praise You, Jesus. I worship You, Jesus. Thank You, Holy Spirit. I praise You, Holy Spirit. I worship You, Holy Spirit.
Amen.

> You shall worship the Lord, your God, and I
> will bless your bread and your water,
> and I will take sickness away from among you.
> Exodus 23:25 (NRSV)

Day 218

Before Father God I decree, and I declare in the name of Jesus Christ of Nazareth, that you, *my baby*, have an angel sent before you to guard you on the way and bring you to the place God has prepared for you.

Thank You, Father. I praise You, Father. I worship You, Father. Thank You, Jesus. I praise You, Jesus. I worship You, Jesus. Thank You, Holy Spirit. I praise You, Holy Spirit. I worship You, Holy Spirit.
Amen.

> I am going to send an angel in the front
> of you, to guard you on the way
> and to bring you to the place that I have
> prepared. Exodus 23:20 (NRSV)

Day 219

Before Father God I decree, and I declare in the name of Jesus Christ of Nazareth, that you, *my baby*, will love the Lord and obey his commandments, statutes, and ordinances. You will walk in his ways.

Thank You, Father. I praise You, Father. I worship You, Father. Thank You, Jesus. I praise You, Jesus. I worship You, Jesus. Thank You, Holy Spirit. I praise You, Holy Spirit. I worship You, Holy Spirit.
Amen.

> If you obey the commandments of the LORD,
> your God, … by loving the LORD your God,
> walking in his ways, and observing his
> commandments, decrees, and ordinances,
> then you shall live and become numerous.
> Deuteronomy 30:16 (NRSV)

Day 220

Before Father God I decree, and I declare in the name of Jesus Christ of Nazareth, that you, *my baby*, will live and grow numerous. God will bless you in the land.

Thank You, Father. I praise You, Father. I worship You, Father. Thank You, Jesus. I praise You, Jesus. I worship You, Jesus. Thank You, Holy Spirit. I praise You, Holy Spirit. I worship You, Holy Spirit.
Amen.

> If you obey the commandments of the LORD, your God …
> then you shall live and become numerous,
> and the LORD, your God, will bless you in the
> land that you are entering to possess.
> Deuteronomy 30:16 (NRSV)

Day 221

Before Father God I decree, and I declare in the name of Jesus Christ of Nazareth, that you, *my baby*, will talk to heaven, and the earth will hear your words.

Thank You, Father. I praise You, Father. I worship You, Father. Thank You, Jesus. I praise You, Jesus. I worship You, Jesus. Thank You, Holy Spirit. I praise You, Holy Spirit. I worship You, Holy Spirit.
Amen.

Give ear, O heavens, and I will speak;
let the earth hear the words of my mouth.
Deuteronomy 32:1 (NRSV)

Day 222

Before Father God I decree, and I declare in the name of Jesus Christ of Nazareth, that you, *my baby*, will teach, and your teaching will soak in like the rain and your utterance drench like the dew.

Thank You, Father. I praise You, Father. I worship You, Father. Thank You, Jesus. I praise You, Jesus. I worship You, Jesus. Thank You, Holy Spirit. I praise You, Holy Spirit. I worship You, Holy Spirit.
Amen.

May my teaching drop like the rain, my
speech condense like the dew
like gentle rain on grass, like showers on new growth.
Deuteronomy 32:2 (NRSV)

Day 223

Before Father God I decree, and I declare in the name of Jesus Christ of Nazareth, that you, *my baby*, will proclaim the name of the Lord and praise the greatness of our God.

Thank You, Father. I praise You, Father. I worship You, Father. Thank You, Jesus. I praise You, Jesus. I worship You, Jesus. Thank You, Holy Spirit. I praise You, Holy Spirit. I worship You, Holy Spirit.
Amen.

> For I will proclaim the name of the LORD;
> ascribe greatness of our God!
> Deuteronomy 32:3 (NRSV)

Day 224

Before Father God I decree, and I declare in the name of Jesus Christ of Nazareth, that you, *my baby*, are shielded and cared by God. You are the apple of God's eye.

Thank You, Father. I praise You, Father. I worship You, Father. Thank You, Jesus. I praise You, Jesus. I worship You, Jesus. Thank You, Holy Spirit. I praise You, Holy Spirit. I worship You, Holy Spirit.
Amen.

> He sustain him in a desert land, in a
> howling wilderness waste;
> he shielded him, cared for him, guarded
> him as the apple of his eye.
> Deuteronomy 32:10 (NRSV)

Day 225

Before Father God I decree, and I declare in the name of Jesus Christ of Nazareth, that you, *my baby*, are guided by the Lord.

Thank You, Father. I praise You, Father. I worship You, Father. Thank You, Jesus. I praise You, Jesus. I worship You, Jesus. Thank You, Holy Spirit. I praise You, Holy Spirit. I worship You, Holy Spirit.
Amen.

The LORD alone guided him; no foreign god was with them.
Deuteronomy 32:12 (NRSV)

Day 226

Before Father God I decree, and I declare in the name of Jesus Christ of Nazareth, that you, *my baby*, are a child of God. God blessed your strength. God will be pleased with the work of your hands.

Thank You, Father. I praise You, Father. I worship You, Father. Thank You, Jesus. I praise You, Jesus. I worship You, Jesus. Thank You, Holy Spirit. I praise You, Holy Spirit. I worship You, Holy Spirit.
Amen.

Bless, LORD, his substance, and accept
the work of his hands.
Deuteronomy 33:11 (NRSV

Day 227

Before Father God I decree, and I declare in the name of Jesus Christ of Nazareth, that you, *my baby*, will taste and see that the Lord is good.

Thank You, Father. I praise You, Father. I worship You, Father. Thank You, Jesus. I praise You, Jesus. I worship You, Jesus. Thank You, Holy Spirit. I praise You, Holy Spirit. I worship You, Holy Spirit.
Amen.

O taste and see that the LORD is good.
Psalm 34:8 (NRSV)

Day 228

Before Father God I decree, and I declare in the name of Jesus Christ of Nazareth, that you, *my baby*, will seek the Lord and He will answer you. He will deliver you from all yours fears.

Thank You, Father. I praise You, Father. I worship You, Father. Thank You, Jesus. I praise You, Jesus. I worship You, Jesus. Thank You, Holy Spirit. I praise You, Holy Spirit. I worship You, Holy Spirit.
Amen.

I sought the LORD, and he answered me,
delivered me from all my fears.
Psalm 34:4 (NRSV)

Day 229

Before Father God I decree, and I declare in the name of Jesus Christ of Nazareth, that you, *my baby*, are encamped around by the angel of the Lord. God saves you.

Thank You, Father. I praise You, Father. I worship You, Father. Thank You, Jesus. I praise You, Jesus. I worship You, Jesus. Thank You, Holy Spirit. I praise You, Holy Spirit. I worship You, Holy Spirit.
Amen.

> The angel of the LORD encamps around those
> who fear him, and delivers them.
> Psalm 34:7 (NRSV)

Day 230

Before Father God I decree, and I declare in the name of Jesus Christ of Nazareth, that you, *my baby*, are blessed. God Almighty will help you. You are blessed with blessings from the heavens above.

Thank You, Father. I praise You, Father. I worship You, Father. Thank You, Jesus. I praise You, Jesus. I worship You, Jesus. Thank You, Holy Spirit. I praise You, Holy Spirit. I worship You, Holy Spirit.
Amen.

> By the God of your father, who will help you,
> by the Almighty, who will blesses you,
> with blessings of heaven above,
> blessings of the deep that lies beneath,
> blessings of the breasts and of the womb.
> Genesis 49:25 (NRSV)

Day 231

Before Father God I decree, and I declare in the name of Jesus Christ of Nazareth, that you, *my baby*, are blessed. The Lord's face shines upon you. The Lord is gracious to you.

Thank You, Father. I praise You, Father. I worship You, Father. Thank You, Jesus. I praise You, Jesus. I worship You, Jesus. Thank You, Holy Spirit. I praise You, Holy Spirit. I worship You, Holy Spirit.
Amen.

> The Lord bless you and keep you:
> the Lord make his face shine upon
> you, and be gracious to you.
> Numbers 6:24-25 (NRSV)

Day 232

Before Father God I decree, and I declare in the name of Jesus Christ of Nazareth, that you, *my baby*, have received power from God to get wealth.

Thank You, Father. I praise You, Father. I worship You, Father. Thank You, Jesus. I praise You, Jesus. I worship You, Jesus. Thank You, Holy Spirit. I praise You, Holy Spirit. I worship You, Holy Spirit.
Amen.

> But remember the Lord your God, for it is he
> who gives you power to get wealth.
> Deuteronomy 8:18 (NRSV)

Day 233

Before Father God I decree, and I declare in the name of Jesus Christ of Nazareth, that you, *my baby*, put your hope and trust in the Lord from your youth.

Thank You, Father. I praise You, Father. I worship You, Father. Thank You, Jesus. I praise You, Jesus. I worship You, Jesus. Thank You, Holy Spirit. I praise You, Holy Spirit. I worship You, Holy Spirit.
Amen.

> For you, O Lord are my hope,
> my trust, O Lord, from my youth.
> Psalm 71:5 (NRSV)

Day 234

Before Father God I decree, and I declare in the name of Jesus Christ of Nazareth, that you, my baby, are blessed. Your mouth is filled with the Lord's praises. You will sing the Lord's glory every day.

Thank You, Father. I praise You, Father. I worship You, Father. Thank You, Jesus. I praise You, Jesus. I worship You, Jesus. Thank You, Holy Spirit. I praise You, Holy Spirit. I worship You, Holy Spirit.
Amen.

> My mouth is filled with your praises,
> and with your glory all day long.
> Psalm 71:8 (NRSV)

Day 235

Before Father God I decree, and I declare in the name of Jesus Christ of Nazareth, that you, *my baby*, will know wisdom and discipline.

Thank You, Father. I praise You, Father. I worship You, Father. Thank You, Jesus. I praise You, Jesus. I worship You, Jesus. Thank You, Holy Spirit. I praise You, Holy Spirit. I worship You, Holy Spirit.
Amen.

> For learning about wisdom and instruction,
> for understanding words of insight.
> Proverbs 1:2 (NRSV)

Day 236

Before Father God I decree, and I declare in the name of Jesus Christ of Nazareth, that you, *my baby*, will receive instruction in wise conduct, in what is right, just, and fair.

Thank You, Father. I praise You, Father. I worship You, Father. Thank You, Jesus. I praise You, Jesus. I worship You, Jesus. Thank You, Holy Spirit. I praise You, Holy Spirit. I worship You, Holy Spirit.
Amen.

> For gaining instruction in wise dealing,
> righteousness, justice, and equity.
> Proverbs 1:3 (NRSV)

Day 237

Before Father God I decree, and I declare in the name of Jesus Christ of Nazareth, that you, *my baby*, will bless those who prosecute you. You will bless and not curse them.

Thank You, Father. I praise You, Father. I worship You, Father. Thank You, Jesus. I praise You, Jesus. I worship You, Jesus. Thank You, Holy Spirit. I praise You, Holy Spirit. I worship You, Holy Spirit.
Amen.

> Bless those who persecute you; bless
> and do not curse them.
> Romans 12:14 (NRSV)

Day 238

Before Father God I decree, and I declare in the name of Jesus Christ of Nazareth, that you, *my baby*, will live at peace with all.

Thank You, Father. I praise You, Father. I worship You, Father. Thank You, Jesus. I praise You, Jesus. I worship You, Jesus. Thank You, Holy Spirit. I praise You, Holy Spirit. I worship You, Holy Spirit.
Amen.

> If it is possible, so far as it depends on
> you, live at peaceably with all.
> Romans 12:18 (NRSV)

Day 239

Before Father God I decree, and I declare in the name of Jesus Christ of Nazareth, that you, *my baby*, will conquer evil with good.

Thank You, Father. I praise You, Father. I worship You, Father. Thank You, Jesus. I praise You, Jesus. I worship You, Jesus. Thank You, Holy Spirit. I praise You, Holy Spirit. I worship You, Holy Spirit.
Amen.

Do not be overcome by evil, but overcome evil with good.
Romans 12:21 (NRSV)

Day 240

Before Father God I decree, and I declare in the name of Jesus Christ of Nazareth, that you, *my baby*, will put on the Lord Jesus Christ every day.

Thank You, Father. I praise You, Father. I worship You, Father. Thank You, Jesus. I praise You, Jesus. I worship You, Jesus. Thank You, Holy Spirit. I praise You, Holy Spirit. I worship You, Holy Spirit.
Amen.

Instead, put on the Lord Jesus Christ,
and make no provision
for the flesh, to gratify its desire.
Romans 13:14 (NRSV)

Day 241

Before Father God I decree, and I declare in the name of Jesus Christ of Nazareth, that you, *my baby*, will live every day for the Lord. You belong to the Lord.

Thank You, Father. I praise You, Father. I worship You, Father. Thank You, Jesus. I praise You, Jesus. I worship You, Jesus. Thank You, Holy Spirit. I praise You, Holy Spirit. I worship You, Holy Spirit.
Amen.

> If we live, we live to the Lord, and if
> we die, we die to the Lord;
> so then, whether we live or whether
> we die, we are the Lord's.
> Romans 14:8 (NRSV)

Day 242

Before Father God I decree, and I declare in the name of Jesus Christ of Nazareth, that you, *my baby*, are blessed. The God of hope will fill you with all joy and peace in believing, so that you may abound in hope by the power of the Holy Spirit.

Thank You, Father. I praise You, Father. I worship You, Father. Thank You, Jesus. I praise You, Jesus. I worship You, Jesus. Thank You, Holy Spirit. I praise You, Holy Spirit. I worship You, Holy Spirit.
Amen.

> May the God of hope fill you with all
> joy and peace in believing,
> so that you may abound in hope by
> the power of the Holy Spirit.
> Romans 15:13 (NRSV)

Day 243

Before Father God I decree, and I declare in the name of Jesus Christ of Nazareth, that you, *my baby*, are full of goodness and will be filled with all knowledge.

Thank You, Father. I praise You, Father. I worship You, Father. Thank You, Jesus. I praise You, Jesus. I worship You, Jesus. Thank You, Holy Spirit. I praise You, Holy Spirit. I worship You, Holy Spirit.
Amen.

> I myself feel confident about you,
> my brothers and my sister,
> that you yourselves are full of goodness,
> filled with all knowledge,
> and able to instruct one another.
> Romans 15:14 (NRSV)

Day 244

Before Father God I decree, and I declare in the name of Jesus Christ of Nazareth, that you, *my baby*, are blessed. In all your ways, be mindful of the Lord, and the Lord will make straight your paths.

Thank You, Father. I praise You, Father. I worship You, Father. Thank You, Jesus. I praise You, Jesus. I worship You, Jesus. Thank You, Holy Spirit. I praise You, Holy Spirit. I worship You, Holy Spirit.
Amen.

> In all your ways acknowledge him,
> and he will make straight your paths.
> Proverbs 3:6 (NRSV)

Day 245

Before Father God I decree, and I declare in the name of Jesus Christ of Nazareth, that you, *my baby*, will honor the Lord with your wealth and with firstfruits of all that you produce in abundance. Your barns will be filled with plenty, and with new wine your vats will overflow.

Thank You, Father. I praise You, Father. I worship You, Father.
Thank You, Jesus. I praise You, Jesus. I worship You, Jesus.
Thank You, Holy Spirit. I praise You, Holy Spirit. I worship You, Holy Spirit.
Amen.

> Honor the LORD with your substance
> and with the first fruits of all your produce;
> then your barns will be filled with plenty,
> and your vast will be bursting with wine.
> Proverbs 3:9–10 (NRSV)

Day 246

Before Father God I decree, and I declare in the name of Jesus Christ of Nazareth, that you, *my baby*, have been filled with wisdom. You have long life in your right hand and riches and honor in your left.

Thank You, Father. I praise You, Father. I worship You, Father.
Thank You, Jesus. I praise You, Jesus. I worship You, Jesus.
Thank You, Holy Spirit. I praise You, Holy Spirit. I worship You, Holy Spirit.
Amen.

> Long life is in her right hand,
> in her left are riches and honor.
> Proverbs 3:16 (NRSV)

Day 247

Before Father God I decree, and I declare in the name of Jesus Christ of Nazareth, that you, *my baby*, are blessed. When you sit down, you will not be afraid. When you rest, your sleep will be sweet.

Thank You, Father. I praise You, Father. I worship You, Father. Thank You, Jesus. I praise You, Jesus. I worship You, Jesus. Thank You, Holy Spirit. I praise You, Holy Spirit. I worship You, Holy Spirit.
Amen.

> If you sit down, you will not be afraid,
> when you lie down, your sleep will be sweet.
> Proverbs 3:24 (NRSV)

Day 248

Before Father God I decree, and I declare in the name of Jesus Christ of Nazareth, that you, *my baby*, will be diligent and your appetite will be amply satisfied.

Thank You, Father. I praise You, Father. I worship You, Father. Thank You, Jesus. I praise You, Jesus. I worship You, Jesus. Thank You, Holy Spirit. I praise You, Holy Spirit. I worship You, Holy Spirit.
Amen.

> Proverbs 13:4 (NRSV)
> The appetite of the lazy craves, and gets nothing,
> while the appetite of the diligent is richly satisfied.

Day 249

Before Father God I decree, and I declare in the name of Jesus Christ of Nazareth, that you, *my baby*, are happy because you trust the Lord. You will ponder His word and you will be successful.

Thank You, Father. I praise You, Father. I worship You, Father. Thank You, Jesus. I praise You, Jesus. I worship You, Jesus. Thank You, Holy Spirit. I praise You, Holy Spirit. I worship You, Holy Spirit.
Amen.

> Those who are attentive to a matter will prosper,
> and happy are those who trusts in the Lord!
> Proverbs 16:20 (NRSV)

Day 250

Before Father God I decree, and I declare in the name of Jesus Christ of Nazareth, that you, *my baby*, will always entrust your works to the Lord, and your plans will succeed.

Thank You, Father. I praise You, Father. I worship You, Father. Thank You, Jesus. I praise You, Jesus. I worship You, Jesus. Thank You, Holy Spirit. I praise You, Holy Spirit. I worship You, Holy Spirit.
Amen.

> Commit your works to the Lord,
> and your plans will be established.
> Proverbs 16:3 (NRSV)

Day 251

Before Father God I decree, and I declare in the name of Jesus Christ of Nazareth, that you, *my baby*, are blessed and all the Lord's plans for you will endure.

Thank You, Father. I praise You, Father. I worship You, Father. Thank You, Jesus. I praise You, Jesus. I worship You, Jesus. Thank You, Holy Spirit. I praise You, Holy Spirit. I worship You, Holy Spirit.
Amen.

> The human mind may devise many plans,
> but it is the purpose of the LORD
> that will be established.
> Proverbs 19:21 (NRSV)

Day 252

Before Father God I decree, and I declare in the name of Jesus Christ of Nazareth, that you, *my baby*, are blessed. Your home is built by wisdom and established by understanding. Knowledge fills the rooms with every precious and pleasing possession.

Thank You, Father. I praise You, Father. I worship You, Father. Thank You, Jesus. I praise You, Jesus. I worship You, Jesus. Thank You, Holy Spirit. I praise You, Holy Spirit. I worship You, Holy Spirit.
Amen.

> By wisdom a house is built,
> and by understanding it is established;
> by knowledge the rooms are filled
> with all precious and pleasant riches.
> Proverbs 24:3-4 (NRSV)

Day 253

Before Father God I decree, and I declare in the name of Jesus Christ of Nazareth, that you, *my baby*, are wise and more powerful than the strong one.

Thank You, Father. I praise You, Father. I worship You, Father. Thank You, Jesus. I praise You, Jesus. I worship You, Jesus. Thank You, Holy Spirit. I praise You, Holy Spirit. I worship You, Holy Spirit.
Amen.

> Wise warriors are mightier than strong ones,
> and those who have knowledge than
> those who have strength.
> Proverbs 24:5 (NRSV)

Day 254

Before Father God I decree, and I declare in the name of Jesus Christ of Nazareth, that you, *my baby*, are blessed. Wisdom will enter into your heart, and knowledge will be at home in your soul.

Thank You, Father. I praise You, Father. I worship You, Father. Thank You, Jesus. I praise You, Jesus. I worship You, Jesus. Thank You, Holy Spirit. I praise You, Holy Spirit. I worship You, Holy Spirit.
Amen.

> For wisdom will come into your heart,
> and knowledge will be pleasant to your soul.
> Proverbs 2:10 (NRSV)

Day 255

Before Father God I decree, and I declare in the name of Jesus Christ of Nazareth, that you, *my baby*, are blessed. Discretion will watch over you, and understanding will guard you.

Thank You, Father. I praise You, Father. I worship You, Father. Thank You, Jesus. I praise You, Jesus. I worship You, Jesus. Thank You, Holy Spirit. I praise You, Holy Spirit. I worship You, Holy Spirit.
Amen.

Proverbs 2:11 (NRSV)
Prudence will watch over you,
and understanding will guard you.

Day 256

Before Father God I decree, and I declare in the name of Jesus Christ of Nazareth, that you, *my baby*, will win favor and esteem before God and people.

Thank You, Father. I praise You, Father. I worship You, Father. Thank You, Jesus. I praise You, Jesus. I worship You, Jesus. Thank You, Holy Spirit. I praise You, Holy Spirit. I worship You, Holy Spirit.
Amen.

So you will find favor and good repute
in the sight of God and of people.
Proverbs 3:4 (NRSV)

Day 257

Before Father God I decree, and I declare in the name of Jesus Christ of Nazareth, that you, *my baby*, are God's servant. The Lord delights in the peace and prosperity of his loyal servant.

Thank You, Father. I praise You, Father. I worship You, Father. Thank You, Jesus. I praise You, Jesus. I worship You, Jesus. Thank You, Holy Spirit. I praise You, Holy Spirit. I worship You, Holy Spirit.
Amen.

> Let those who desire my vindication,
> shout for joy and be glad,
> and say evermore "Great is the LORD
> who delights in the welfare of his servant."
> Psalm 35:27 (NRSV)

Day 258

Before Father God I decree, and I declare in the name of Jesus Christ of Nazareth, that you, *my baby*, are blessed. The Lord has granted you salvation along with good fortune and success.

Thank You, Father. I praise You, Father. I worship You, Father. Thank You, Jesus. I praise You, Jesus. I worship You, Jesus. Thank You, Holy Spirit. I praise You, Holy Spirit. I worship You, Holy Spirit.
Amen.

> Save us, we beseech you, O Lord!
> O Lord, we beseech you, give us success!
> Psalm 118:25 (NRSV)

Day 259

Before Father God I decree, and I declare in the name of Jesus Christ of Nazareth, that you, *my baby*, will live in the day the Lord has made. You will rejoice in it and be glad.

Thank You, Father. I praise You, Father. I worship You, Father. Thank You, Jesus. I praise You, Jesus. I worship You, Jesus. Thank You, Holy Spirit. I praise You, Holy Spirit. I worship You, Holy Spirit.
Amen.

> This is the day the Lord has made; let
> us rejoice in it and be glad.
> Psalm 118:24 (NRSV)

Day 260

Before Father God I decree, and I declare in the name of Jesus Christ of Nazareth, that you, *my baby*, are God's child. The Lord will make His ways known to you. The Lord will teach you His paths.

Thank You, Father. I praise You, Father. I worship You, Father. Thank You, Jesus. I praise You, Jesus. I worship You, Jesus. Thank You, Holy Spirit. I praise You, Holy Spirit. I worship You, Holy Spirit.
Amen.

> Make me to know your ways, Lord;
> teach me your paths.
> Psalm 25:4 (NRSV)

Day 261

Before Father God I decree, and I declare in the name of Jesus Christ of Nazareth, that you, *my baby*, are God's child. Integrity and uprightness will preserve you because you wait for the Lord.

Thank You, Father. I praise You, Father. I worship You, Father. Thank You, Jesus. I praise You, Jesus. I worship You, Jesus. Thank You, Holy Spirit. I praise You, Holy Spirit. I worship You, Holy Spirit.
Amen.

> May integrity and uprightness preserve me;
> for I wait for you.
> Psalm 25:21 (NRSV)

Day 262

Before Father God I decree, and I declare in the name of Jesus Christ of Nazareth, that you, *my baby*, will spent your days in prosperity and your years in happiness because you listen and serve Him.

Thank You, Father. I praise You, Father. I worship You, Father. Thank You, Jesus. I praise You, Jesus. I worship You, Jesus. Thank You, Holy Spirit. I praise You, Holy Spirit. I worship You, Holy Spirit.
Amen.

> If they listen, and serve him,
> they complete their days in prosperity,
> and their years in pleasantness.
> Job 36:11 (NRSV)

Day 263

Before Father God I decree, and I declare in the name of Jesus Christ of Nazareth, that you, *my baby*, are God's child. God formed your inmost being and knit you in the womb.

Thank You, Father. I praise You, Father. I worship You, Father. Thank You, Jesus. I praise You, Jesus. I worship You, Jesus. Thank You, Holy Spirit. I praise You, Holy Spirit. I worship You, Holy Spirit.
Amen.

Psalm 139:13 (NRSV)
For it was you who formed my inward parts;
you knit me together in my mother's womb.

Day 264

Before Father God I decree, and I declare in the name of Jesus Christ of Nazareth, that you, *my baby*, are fearfully and wonderfully made.

Thank You, Father. I praise You, Father. I worship You, Father. Thank You, Jesus. I praise You, Jesus. I worship You, Jesus. Thank You, Holy Spirit. I praise You, Holy Spirit. I worship You, Holy Spirit.
Amen.

I praise you, for I am fearfully and wonderfully made.
Wonderful are your works;
that I know very well.
Psalm 139:14 (NRSV)

Day 265

Before Father God I decree, and I declare in the name of Jesus Christ of Nazareth, that you, *my baby*, are God's child. Your bones were not hidden from God when you were being made in secret, fashioned in the depths of the earth.

Thank You, Father. I praise You, Father. I worship You, Father. Thank You, Jesus. I praise You, Jesus. I worship You, Jesus. Thank You, Holy Spirit. I praise You, Holy Spirit. I worship You, Holy Spirit.
Amen.

> My frame was not hidden from you,
> when I was being made in secret,
> intricately woven in the depths of the earth.
> Psalm 139: 15 (NRSV)

Day 266

Before Father God I decree, and I declare in the name of Jesus Christ of Nazareth, that you, *my baby*, belong to God. He saw you unformed. He shaped all your days and wrote the book of your life.

Thank You, Father. I praise You, Father. I worship You, Father. Thank You, Jesus. I praise You, Jesus. I worship You, Jesus. Thank You, Holy Spirit. I praise You, Holy Spirit. I worship You, Holy Spirit.
Amen.

> Your eyes beheld my unformed substance.
> In your book were written
> all the days that were formed for me,
> when none of them as yet existed.
> Psalm 139:16 (NRSV)

Day 267

Before Father God I decree, and I declare in the name of Jesus Christ of Nazareth, that you, *my baby*, will have visions. Angels will come and speak with you.

Thank You, Father. I praise You, Father. I worship You, Father. Thank You, Jesus. I praise You, Jesus. I worship You, Jesus. Thank You, Holy Spirit. I praise You, Holy Spirit. I worship You, Holy Spirit.
Amen.

One afternoon at about three o'clock, he
had vision in which he clearly saw
an angel of God coming in and [speaking his name] to him.
Acts 10:3 (NRSV)

Day 268

Before Father God I decree, and I declare in the name of Jesus Christ of Nazareth, that you, *my baby*, are God's child. God has commanded His angels to guard you whenever you go.

Thank You, Father. I praise You, Father. I worship You, Father. Thank You, Jesus. I praise You, Jesus. I worship You, Jesus. Thank You, Holy Spirit. I praise You, Holy Spirit. I worship You, Holy Spirit.
Amen.

For he will command his angeis concerning you,
to guard you in all your ways.
Psalm 91:11 (NRSV)

Day 269

Before Father God I decree, and I declare in the name of Jesus Christ of Nazareth, that you, *my baby*, are called by name by the God of Israel. He will give you hidden treasure.

Thank You, Father. I praise You, Father. I worship You, Father. Thank You, Jesus. I praise You, Jesus. I worship You, Jesus. Thank You, Holy Spirit. I praise You, Holy Spirit. I worship You, Holy Spirit.
Amen.

> I will give you the treasure of darkness
> and riches hidden in secret places,
> so that you may know that it is I, the LORD, the God of Israel,
> who call you by your name.
> Isaiah 45:3 (NRSV)

Day 270

Before Father God I decree, and I declare in the name of Jesus Christ of Nazareth, that you, *my baby*, are blessed. God will pour His Spirit upon your offspring and His blessing upon your descendants.

Thank You, Father. I praise You, Father. I worship You, Father. Thank You, Jesus. I praise You, Jesus. I worship You, Jesus. Thank You, Holy Spirit. I praise You, Holy Spirit. I worship You, Holy Spirit.
Amen.

> For I will pour water on the thirsty land,
> and streams on the dry ground;
> I will pour my spirit upon your descendants,
> and my blessing on your offspring.
> Isaiah 44:3 (NRSV)

Day 271

Before Father God I decree, and I declare in the name of Jesus Christ of Nazareth, that you, *my baby*, are truly blessed by the God of Israel. God extends your boundaries. God's hand is with you and will free you of misfortune.

Thank You, Father. I praise You, Father. I worship You, Father. Thank You, Jesus. I praise You, Jesus. I worship You, Jesus. Thank You, Holy Spirit. I praise You, Holy Spirit. I worship You, Holy Spirit.
Amen.

[He] called on the God of Israel, saying "Oh, that
you would bless me and enlarge my border
and that your hand might be with me
and that you would keep me from hurt and harm!"
And God granted what he asked.
1 Chronicles 4:10 (NRSV)

Day 272

Before Father God I decree, and I declare in the name of Jesus Christ of Nazareth, that you, *my baby*, will build the house for the name of the Lord, the God of Israel.

Thank You, Father. I praise You, Father. I worship You, Father. Thank You, Jesus. I praise You, Jesus. I worship You, Jesus. Thank You, Holy Spirit. I praise You, Holy Spirit. I worship You, Holy Spirit.
Amen.

Now the Lord has fulfilled his promise that he made;
for I ... have built the house for the name
of the Lord, the God of Israel.
2 Chronicles 6:10 (NRSV)

Day 273

Before Father God I decree, and I declare in the name of Jesus Christ of Nazareth, that you, *my baby*, will bless the Lord, who was pleased with you.

Thank You, Father. I praise You, Father. I worship You, Father.
Thank You, Jesus. I praise You, Jesus. I worship You, Jesus.
Thank You, Holy Spirit. I praise You, Holy Spirit. I worship You, Holy Spirit.
Amen.

Blessed be the LORD, your God, who has delighted in you.
2 Chronicles 9:8 (NRSV)

Day 274

Before Father God I decree, and I declare in the name of Jesus Christ of Nazareth, that you, *my baby*, are king and will carry out judgment and justice.

Thank You, Father. I praise You, Father. I worship You, Father.
Thank You, Jesus. I praise You, Jesus. I worship You, Jesus.
Thank You, Holy Spirit. I praise You, Holy Spirit. I worship You, Holy Spirit.
Amen.

God ... has set you on his throne as
king for the LORD, your God ...
He has made you king over them, so that you
may execute justice and righteousness.
2 Chronicles 9:8 (NRSV)

Day 275

Before Father God I decree, and I declare in the name of Jesus Christ of Nazareth, that you, *my baby*, are encouraged by the Lord. He sees that you will be devoted to Him wholeheartedly.

Thank You, Father. I praise You, Father. I worship You, Father. Thank You, Jesus. I praise You, Jesus. I worship You, Jesus. Thank You, Holy Spirit. I praise You, Holy Spirit. I worship You, Holy Spirit.
Amen.

For the eyes of the LORD range throughout the entire earth,
to strengthen those whose heart is true to him.
2 Chronicles 16:9 (NRSV)

Day 276

Before Father God I decree, and I declare in the name of Jesus Christ of Nazareth, that you, *my baby*, will have firm faith in the Lord. You will believe the prophets, and you will succeed.

Thank You, Father. I praise You, Father. I worship You, Father. Thank You, Jesus. I praise You, Jesus. I worship You, Jesus. Thank You, Holy Spirit. I praise You, Holy Spirit. I worship You, Holy Spirit.
Amen.

Believe in the LORD, your God and you will
be established; believe his prophets.
2 Chronicles 20:20 (NRSV)

Day 277

Before Father God I decree, and I declare in the name of Jesus Christ of Nazareth, that you, *my baby*, will give thanks, praises, and worship to the Lord, whose love endures forever.

Thank You, Father. I praise You, Father. I worship You, Father. Thank You, Jesus. I praise You, Jesus. I worship You, Jesus. Thank You, Holy Spirit. I praise You, Holy Spirit. I worship You, Holy Spirit.
Amen.

> "Give thanks to the LORD, for his
> steadfast love endues forever."
> 2 Chronicles 20:21 (NRSV)

Day 278

Before Father God I decree, and I declare in the name of Jesus Christ of Nazareth, that you, *my baby*, have been given joy over your enemies.

Thank You, Father. I praise You, Father. I worship You, Father. Thank You, Jesus. I praise You, Jesus. I worship You, Jesus. Thank You, Holy Spirit. I praise You, Holy Spirit. I worship You, Holy Spirit.
Amen.

> Then all the people of Judah and Jerusalem …
> returned to Jerusalem with joy;
> for the LORD had enabled them to rejoice over their enemies
> 2 Chronicles 20:27 (NRSV)

Day 279

Before Father God I decree, and I declare in the name of Jesus Christ of Nazareth, that you, *my baby*, are blessed. Whatever you ask in Jesus's name, Jesus will do it, so that the Father may be glorified in the Son.

Thank You, Father. I praise You, Father. I worship You, Father. Thank You, Jesus. I praise You, Jesus. I worship You, Jesus. Thank You, Holy Spirit. I praise You, Holy Spirit. I worship You, Holy Spirit.
Amen.

> I [Jesus] will do whatever you ask in my name,
> so that the Father may be glorified in the Son.
> John 14:13 (NRSV)

Day 280

Before Father God I decree, and I declare in the name of Jesus Christ of Nazareth, that you, *my baby*, will ask and it will be given to you. You will seek and you will find. You will knock and the door will open to you.

Thank You, Father. I praise You, Father. I worship You, Father. Thank You, Jesus. I praise You, Jesus. I worship You, Jesus. Thank You, Holy Spirit. I praise You, Holy Spirit. I worship You, Holy Spirit.
Amen.

> Ask, and it will be given to you; search, and you will find;
> knock, and the door will be opened to you.
> Matthew 7:7 (NRSV)

Welcome to the world …

Printed in the United States
by Baker & Taylor Publisher Services